TRIALS TO
TRIUMPHS

*Perspectives from
Successful Healthcare Leaders*

TRIALS TO TRIUMPHS

Perspectives from Successful Healthcare Leaders

Edited by
Donald J. Lloyd,
Donald C. Wegmiller,
and W. Robert Wright, Jr.

ACHE Management Series
Health Administration Press, Chicago, Illinois

Your board staff or clients may benefit from this book's insight. For more information on quantity discounts, contact the Health Administration Press Marketing Manager at (312) 424–9470.

05 04 03 02 01   5   4   3   2   1

Library of Congress Cataloging-in-Publication Data

Trials to triumphs : perspectives from successful healthcare leaders / edited by Donald J. Lloyd, Donald C. Wegmiller, W. Robert Wright, Jr.
    p. cm.
    ISBN 1-56793-151-0
    1. Health services administrators. 2. Leadership. I. Lloyd, Donald J. II. Wegmiller, Donald C. III. Wright, W. Robert.
RA971 .T75 2001
362.1'068'4—dc21   2001016721

The paper used in this publication meets the minimum requirements of American National Standard for Information Sciences—Permanence of Paper for Printed Library Materials, ANSI Z39.48–1984.™

Project manager: Cami Cacciatore; Book design: Matt Avery; Cover design: Anne LoCascio

Health Administration Press
A division of the Foundation of the
    American College of Healthcare Executives
1 North Franklin Street, Suite 1700
Chicago, IL 60606–3491
(312) 424–2800

To my friends and colleagues in group practice administration. I sincerely thank you for a lifetime of support and encouragement.

—Donald J. Lloyd

To the future leaders of healthcare organizations that 'do the right things for the right reasons' . . . that they maintain the passion to make a difference.

—W. Robert Wright, Jr.

This book is dedicated to the University of Minnesota Program in Health Care Administration and all of its alumni. By providing them with an excellent educational experience, the program has produced individuals who have gone on to become healthcare leaders in this country.

—Donald C. Wegmiller

CONTENTS

Acknowledgments

The editors wish to express our sincere appreciation to the 61 eminent healthcare leaders who participated in this project. Each of them graciously took a personal risk by allowing us to take a snapshot of their thought processes, struggles, and frailties as they built successful careers as medical executives. They did so in the hope that their experiences might make a difference to colleagues and aspiring young leaders. We're convinced that their contributions will have a positive and lasting impact.

We also want to thank the many staff members of Health Administration Press for their support and advice during the production of this work. Without their tireless efforts, we could not have completed the project.

Finally, we want to acknowledge Rob Fromberg, a friend and former associate director at Health Administration Press, for coordinating our efforts and keeping us on target. He was the glue that kept the project together.

Introduction

"The credit belongs to the man who is actually in the arena; whose face is marred by dust and sweat and blood; who strives valiantly; who errs and comes short again and again; who knows the great enthusiasms, the great devotions, and spends himself in a worthy cause; who at the best knows in the end the triumph of high achievement; and who at the worst, if he fails, at least fails while daring greatly. . . ." —Theodore Roosevelt

THE HEALTHCARE REVOLUTION that began over a decade ago continues unabated as we move into the early years of the third millennium. This is unwelcome news for those who thought that the simple turn of a page on the calendar would restore stability to the financing and delivery of healthcare. In fact, our industry is changing at an ever-increasing rate.

So, if this is true, why should we even want to consider the past as we move at warp speed into the future? The answer is that the past is prologue for the future. Yes, the issues themselves can be instructive, but it is the process of problem solving and the mindset of past leaders that provide the real lessons. Our purpose in putting together a book of "war stories" was to demonstrate to our colleagues that career success does not mean the absence of adversity, self-doubt, or disappointment. Rather, it was to illustrate that long-term success results from learning from our mistakes . . . and those of others, as well as persevering through the uncertainty that confronts us on a regular basis.

We hope this book will provide a pathway for you as it offers the wisdom of respected executives who have been down the road before you. At some time in your career, you may actually face the exact challenge outlined in one of our leader's stories. If so, that's a bonus. You will, however, undoubtedly be faced with having to confront some difficult situations, career decisions, and personal challenges along the way. It is by studying how our veteran executives handled these challenges that you will find what we believe are the guiding lights of healthcare management and leadership. Their narratives will offer you valuable insights, advice, and even inspiration as they recount the trials they have faced in long and productive careers. Over 60 distinguished individuals were gracious enough to share their experiences with us. As hard as it is to comprehend, their combined careers represent nearly *fifteen hundred years* of healthcare experience.

Our prominent contributors were asked to briefly articulate a significant *operational, strategic, relationship,* or *career* challenge, placing particular emphasis on the thought process they used in dealing with the situation or event. We also requested that they summarize some lessons learned from the experience. The results were beyond our most optimistic expectations. What these leaders offer are their own stories—sometimes very personal stories—of how they have dealt with some of their most daunting professional challenges. We not only get to see how they solved their problems and dealt with adversity, but we often see apprehension and self-doubt. This is very instructive because they are just like us, sometimes stumbling along the way, but ultimately recovering to master their world.

Included are leaders from hospitals, health systems, medical group practices, various healthcare associations, academia, and public policy groups. Many are physicians, some are lay medical administrators, still others are entrepreneurs, and a few are from the academic or government arenas. This rare mosaic of perspectives provides a clear picture of how to succeed in the complex world of healthcare management and leadership. There is literally something for every one of us who aspires to excel in our chosen field.

The stories are as diverse as the contributors. You will see how our leaders dealt with career decisions, change management, ethical issues, building and maintaining positive working relationships, power struggles, embezzlement, organizational development, creating a new culture, team building, entrepreneurial opportunities, mergers and integration, and termination. They are not only interesting to read, but often very poignant.

The lessons are simple, yet profound. To succeed as a leader you must focus on issues bigger than yourself. You must possess the foresight to recognize opportunities and threats as they develop— not after they are in full bloom. You must learn from the experiences of others. You must understand your own abilities and limitations and surround yourself with capable and loyal associates. Finally, and perhaps most importantly, you must believe in yourself and maintain a positive attitude.

No career in leadership is without its trials and tribulations because there is no perfect world. We can all look forward to facing difficult events, uncertainty, ego deflation, and many other setbacks in our professional lives. We might as well accept the realities and embrace these challenges, because, you see, it is how we deal with these character tests that separate us from the pack, and how well we do it that determines whether or not we can convert them from trials to triumphs!

PART I

STRATEGY

Introduction

STRATEGY, THE ART or skill of using tactics and strat-
agems to achieve goals, is usually developed through experience.
Another method for honing and improving your own strategic abilities
is to observe how other executives have developed strategies to attain
their goals.

To that end, this section of *Trials to Triumphs* shares real life examples of how successful executives identified and dealt with significant
strategic challenges to their organizations. These case studies cover
strategic issues in five categories:

* Dealing with issues related to payers
* Challenges relating to multihospital systems
* Hospital and physician integration
* Challenges faced by healthcare associations
* Issues surrounding the mission of an organization

ISSUES RELATED TO PAYERS

* F. Kenneth Ackerman, Jr., describes the development of the
  Geisinger Health Plan, one of the very early provider-sponsored
  HMOS, during his tenure as a senior executive at Geisinger Medical
  Center. He believes that "the secret to organizational prosperity is
  having vision and being willing to take calculated risks."

- Reginald M. Ballantyne III, describes how the mission of the PMH Health Resources organization drove them to a successful Medicaid managed care program in Arizona and encourages others to "be sure the requisite skills, abilities, and resources are not only available, but in place at the very outset."
- Earl J. Frederick, president emeritus of Children's Memorial Hospital in Chicago, describes the strategy he employed to deal with severe underfunding of the five children's hospitals serving Illinois' Medicaid children. He advises readers to "accept that it may not always be possible to solve each problem you face from within your own organization."
- Joseph W. Mitlyng, Jr., describes his experience as the chief operating officer of a very large, multispecialty group practice with a majority ownership in a managed care plan in Minneapolis–St. Paul. He describes the strategy employed in dealing with the health plan in order to achieve adequate reimbursement for the group practice, noting that "people pay more for perceived quality."

THE CREATION, DEVELOPMENT, OR MANAGEMENT
OF MULTIHOSPITAL SYSTEMS

- John T. Casey recalls the strategies employed in the sale of Presbyterian St. Luke's Health System in Denver to a for-profit hospital management company in the mid-1980s, long before such transactions were common. "The biggest component of our strategy included firm and specific commitments be made and adhered to."
- Maurice W. Elliott of Methodist Healthcare comments on the strategy of acquiring a pediatric hospital and the successful integration of the hospital into an adult healthcare system: "a merger is not successful by accident . . . it takes constant communication and sensitivity to the concerns of the organization being acquired."
- Stanley R. Nelson, former CEO of Henry Ford Health System, describes the strategy used to develop an entire ring of ambulatory care centers in the Detroit suburbs in the 1970s when such centers

were first being considered. His lesson: "Success in any endeavor is dependent on execution even more than strategy or tactics."

- Douglas D. Hawthorne offers a "top ten" list of advice on strategies used in merging two major multihospital systems, advising that "in mergers, people are the most important element."
- Scott S. Parker provides detailed insights into the creation of one of the nation's first multihospital systems, created largely out of a unique new strategy. Of his experience, he says, "every difficult situation has within it an opportunity for creativity if there is a willingness to take risk and innovate—traits that define the successful leader."
- Elliott C. Roberts, Sr., identifies the political issues and strategies surrounding the creation of a public benefit corporation or charity hospital of Louisiana, which resulted in the Louisiana Healthcare Authority. His advice? "Managers and leaders must be flexible to be able to shift gears when external forces warrant."

HOSPITAL AND PHYSICIAN RELATIONSHIPS

- Robert C. Bohlmann recalls the prediction of the "coming of hospitals" as a force in employing physicians during his tenure as president of the Medical Group Management Association, stating that "a group needs to understand and respect its culture. For those groups that don't have a culture, they need to create one."
- Robert L. Goldstein of Summit Health Group describes the creation of the Health Group as a new company, equally owned by physicians and a hospital organization, designed to be a physician-driven but physician-integrated healthcare organization. He quickly learned that "flexibility and agility are the key ingredients in managing a medical group enterprise successfully."
- Robert A. Nelson, currently principal of the Canon Group in California, recalls a history-changing board retreat of the Friendly Hills Medical Group in the mid 1970s where the group decided to enter into its first pre-paid comprehensive contract. He advises, "having leverage is vital to accomplishing difficult tasks. It does

not come without a strong commitment and willingness to take calculated risks."

- Robert J. Wright, current CEO of Medical Cities, Inc., recalls the strategy that led to the creation of Medical City Dallas, one of the nation's most successful "medical malls" combining physician offices and an acute-care hospital all under one roof. "Never stop seeking new and innovative solutions for the needs of your customer. By addressing these needs you will have the opportunity to create."

- Boone Powell, Jr., identifies building and strengthening alliances with its physicians as the number one corporate objective of Baylor Health Care System: "I can say that the smartest way to try and run healthcare organizations today is to find collaborative ways of doing so with your physicians."

LEGISLATIVE ISSUES AND MEMBERSHIP ISSUES

- Dennis S. O'Leary, president of JCAHO, comments on the Commission's current strategy of dealing with the issue of medical errors in healthcare organizations over the last five years. "If there is just cause for a policy—if it is the right thing to do—the organization must be persistent and tenacious in assuring its full and effective implementation."

- Elena C. Rios, president of the National Hispanic Medical Association, recalls the strategy and steps involved in creating the National Hispanic Medical Association. She urges leaders to "have patience and realize that the growth and development of new ideas and/or organizations come in incremental steps that take time."

- John A. Russell, retired CEO of the Hospital Association of Pennsylvania, recalls the strategies employed to deal with the assault on the hospital's tax-exempt status in Pennsylvania during the late 1980s and early 1990s. "The most important events in your career may be crises. How you deal with each crisis determines your management career."

- C. Thomas Smith, Jr., CEO of VHA, Inc., offers this: "If teammates share a common vision and a set of values rooted in personal dignity and mutual respect, then the odds of creating a workable solution are greatly enhanced."

- Margaret E. O'Kane, in creating a new health quality organization, learned to "constantly challenge your own paradigm and be willing to change your thought processes when necessary."
- Karen Ignagni describes her experience as the new president of the American Association of Health Plans and the three initial strategic priorities of the organization. "Success comes from clearly articulating the goals of your organization, and then working toward them."

THE MISSION OF A HEALTHCARE ORGANIZATION

- L. R. (Rush) Jordan describes his attempt to create a community-wide air ambulance service with other providers. The mission of his organization to develop and provide needed community services was the driving force behind the ultimate result. "Make a first-class, good-faith effort to provide the services your community needs."
- Gary A. Mecklenburg tells of how his experience of learning a clear sense of organization mission at a large Catholic hospital served him very well in developing the first strategic plan for a large Chicago academic medical center. "A clearly stated, understood, and actualized sense of mission can be a powerful tool for achieving success."

Whether strategy development deals with the fit of the organization, creation of a new, multihospital system, negotiations with third party payers, integrating physicians into the organization, or leading a healthcare association in its dealings with a diverse set of stakeholders, the challenges of strategy development remain. Rather than face such issues alone and unarmed, let the experience of these successful healthcare leaders guide you as you meet your own strategic challenges.

Strategy

F. Kenneth Ackerman, Jr., FACHE, FACMPE

THIS CASE STUDY spans almost 30 years in the life of the Geisinger Medical Center, based in Danville, Pennsylvania. In retrospect, it seems remarkable that a single, if unheralded, strategic decision so many years ago could have had such an enormous impact on the future of the organization.

Geisinger was a group of roughly 70 physicians located on one site in rural Pennsylvania in the late 1960s when the Nixon administration began to openly discuss the concept of prepaid medicine as a method of expanding coverage and containing costs. At the time, Geisinger was a fee-for-service operation and had no experience with capitated reimbursement.

The leadership of the Medical Center decided, however, to explore the idea of creating our own HMO because we believed it might be an alternative way to finance care and could potentially enhance our attractiveness to our service area in rural northeastern Pennsylvania. There was no grandiose plan, but rather a modest idea for engaging the future.

We initially examined the Kaiser and Ross-Loos HMO models, and even approached one of the Blue Cross plans in Pennsylvania to joint venture the project with us. They declined, and the idea went dormant until 1971 when President Nixon initiated a pilot program to study the efficacy of the HMO concept. We were again intrigued with the idea of "health maintenance" and applied for one of the grants being given to group practices. We also approached Blue Cross again.

This time they accepted, and the Geisinger Health Plan was born in 1973.

In the early years, our members were largely Geisinger staff and a few thousand local residents. Over a 15-year period, the Plan grew to nearly 30,000 members and we finally became solvent.

By the mid-1980s, managed care had fully burst onto the scene, and we were faced with a decision to either close or sell the Plan, or invest major time and resources in it to compete. We chose to make a substantial investment, and by the early 1990s had over 100,000 members. We continued to grow at a rapid pace and quickly crossed the 200,000-member level in the mid-1990s.

Today the Plan has more than 250,000 members and has become one of Geisinger's core business strengths.

The origination of the Plan changed the entire fabric of the Geisinger Health System in ways we simply could not have anticipated:

- The Plan fueled the growth of the organization geographically, requiring more physicians and staff, and the creation of new services. By the late 1990s, Geisinger had grown to over 550 physicians in literally dozens of locations.
- The Plan helped us develop collaborative relationships with physicians and hospitals in other communities around the state.
- The Plan provided a constructive tension within the medical group that encouraged physicians to improve the care delivery process and manage resources more efficiently.
- The Plan promoted us to introduce "physician extenders" into the delivery process, improving access and efficiency.
- The Plan brought us national recognition and notoriety.
- The Plan ultimately became the foundation for the System's marketing efforts.
- The Plan was the catalyst for the introduction of a variety of programs such as smoking cessation, nutrition counseling, and drug and alcohol abuse treatment. It also spurred us to initiate a telephone nurse advice program and a case management process.
- The Plan enabled us to improve every area of clinical and administrative operations.

- Finally, the Plan has been so well managed and operated that it recently received one of 40 citations of excellence by the NCQA.

The strategic decision to embark on the road to prepaid medicine in the early days of development has obviously turned out to be a wise decision. But it did not always appear that this would be the case. We had no idea when we began that it was such a Herculean task to bring an HMO to life and make it financially successful. We struggled tremendously throughout the process and questioned our strategy many times in the first 15 years of existence. There were many times when we paused to consider the Plan's future. Closing it down was always an option. The wisdom was not only in creating the Plan in the early 1970s, but also in believing enough in the concept to continue on into the late 1980s.

Among the most important lessons that we learned from this strategic process were that:

- it requires a committed physician/administrator team to take any idea from inception to reality;
- it takes patience and persistence to make it through the difficult times, particularly when there is tremendous financial strain on the organization;
- organizational growth is energizing and exhilarating for the medical and support staffs, as well as administration; and
- the secret to organizational prosperity is having vision and being willing to take calculated risks.

Success doesn't automatically follow just because a concept is sound. It happens when the leaders of an organization are wise enough to recognize opportunity when it presents itself, and are proactive enough to seize the opportunity when the timing is right.

Mr. Ackerman is a partner and consultant at Healthcare Compensation Strategies in Minneapolis, Minnesota, and was president of the Medical Group Management Association in 1983.

Strategy

Reginald M. Ballantyne III, FACHE

ONE OF THE most difficult strategic problems encountered during my career was at Phoenix Memorial Hospital. We had been serving greater South Phoenix, which includes not only those with insurance, but thousands of people with little or no insurance and no access to healthcare, when healthcare underwent dramatic transformation. The model for providing care for the Medicaid program in Arizona changed. If we did not change with it, our mission-driven rationale to serve all of our community and its neighborhoods would be jeopardized.

In the early- to mid-1980s, managed care organizations were starting to flood the Arizona market and the Medicare Prospective Payment System (PPS) had just arrived when the Medicaid program in Arizona announced its transformation into the Arizona Health Care Cost Containment System (AHCCS). The problem for us was that the AHCCS required a total capitation model. We wanted to treat the Medicaid population; unfortunately, we simply had no experience in the arena of capitated contracts. The message from our board was strong—we had a social responsibility to be in this business. We needed to do whatever it took to fulfill our obligation to serve our patient population.

Our organization decided to take on the challenge and entered the Medicaid managed care market in 1983.

During the first years of the program, PMH suffered financially in this new Medicaid managed care market. Clearly we had underestimated the complexity of the insurance functions and had insufficient understanding of incurred but not reported claims (IBNRs), utilization/case management, and quality assurance for an enrolled population. It became clear that our hospital management team, with its more traditional grasp of reimbursement systems, had neither the background nor skills to cope with the demands of the new market.

We soon recognized that success would mean recruiting experienced specialists, actuaries, managed care managers, and others with a variety of skills. We especially found the insurance/third party aspects of the managed care business were far more complex and important than we had initially comprehended. We engaged our board to develop a framework for success. We also embraced the notion that a strong partnership with the State of Arizona was an essential ingredient for success—not a popular notion at the time.

Our ability to adapt to the changing healthcare environment by doing what it took to be mission driven worked. As a private sector healthcare organization, we found we were able to successfully partner with government to effectively and efficiently serve our patients.

From our experience, we learned the following lessons.

- Actuarial skills, capital reserves, utilization management, and other insurance matters are critical to success.
- The ability to manage in a PMPM (per member per month) market could be relatively easily applied to the PEPM (per employee per month) capitated market in partnership with major employers.
- The traditional executive committee is not the environment in which to conduct economic credentialing of physicians. An independent credentialing activity, which takes into consideration both clinical and economic credentialing, is required.

If I had the opportunity to go back and approach the challenge of entering the managed care marketplace again, we most certainly would do a number of things differently. For example, we would:

- acquire the management team and skills necessary to be successful in advance of entering the managed care business;

- recognize that integration of the delivery and financing of care is an enormous challenge, which to this day is an underestimated hurdle;
- recognize that economic credentialing is not a concept antithetical to clinical care;
- enroll every Medicaid person in the state instead of adopting the "grow it slow" approach, which prevented us from getting to critical mass quickly enough; and
- recognize the power of enrollee choice and create a broader network through contracts with hospitals and physician groups.

We learned that "managed competition" is a solid concept when implemented by knowledgeable healthcare executives in concert with committed physicians. The role of physician involvement in creating and maintaining a successful approach to the management of managed care patients cannot be overemphasized.

We also found the experience gained in dealing with a population enrolled in Medicaid managed care was useful in that it was subsequently applied in our dealings with our commercial market: our insured population.

My final word of advice to other healthcare executives planning on undertaking new initiatives is to be sure the requisite skills, abilities, and resources are not only available, but in place at the very outset.

Mr. Ballantyne is the CEO of PMH Health Resources, Inc. in Pheonix, Arizona and was chairman of the American Hospital Association in 1997.

Strategy

Robert C. Bohlmann, FACMPE

MY CAREER STARTED in the pharmaceutical industry many years ago. I was lucky to have the opportunity to apprentice through various operating units, and in doing so I learned the importance of production, facility design, marketing, public relations, financial management, and the like. Medical group practice management was destined to be my career path.

Over the years, I have been fortunate to work with many talented professionals and be involved in numerous successful organizations. As a rule, I have observed that exceptional professionals with extraordinary focus and vision manage successful organizations. Perhaps it is "the chicken or the egg," in which case I suspect the egg is the enlightened manager. I have observed that talented professionals seem to manage the controllable elements of change and stay one step ahead of the effect of uncontrollable change.

From a professional perspective, one of my finest moments was to have the opportunity to serve as the president of the Medical Group Management Association in 1988. I recall reflecting with the board of directors at the conclusion of an industrious year that medical groups should be aware of the coming of hospitals that were destined to acquire and control medical groups. Well, it did become a reality and it became one of the uncontrollable movements in the evolution of healthcare in the United States. In retrospect, it was a pretty good prediction.

Over the last ten years, we have seen other controlled and uncontrolled changes in medical groups. As an industry, it seems we have tried it all, including a love affair with Wall Street. We have witnessed mergers, acquisitions, divestitures, bankruptcies, and monumental refinements in the financial foundations of health plans and groups. Moreover, regulation and legislation of local, state, and federal government have attempted to influence us to behave differently. And through it all, we have become unhappy, angry, risk averse, and distrustful.

In spite of the turmoil in the world around them, successful medical groups remain. There are lessons to be learned from those thriving groups. From that knowledge is the ability to make others successful as well.

First, a group must truly believe that survival and success can be achieved. They must have the determination to take charge of their destiny and not expect someone else to make it work for them.

Second, a group needs to understand and respect its culture. For those groups that don't have a culture, they need to create one. It needs to be built on a set of core values that will not be compromised for any reason. That means they will not tolerate business relationships, staff, or physicians in the group inconsistent with the group's values.

Third, a group must understand its core business. All decisions should be made with the intent of the core business at the heart of the action. Those groups that describe their core business as "the patient" really get it!

Fourth, a group needs to accept the fact that there is no "free lunch." This translates into a willingness to accept accountability for the decisions they make, the medical care they provide, and the outcomes of that care.

Fifth, I confess to a personal bias that large groups will have a distinct advantage today and into the future. Their advantage resides in their capacity to positively influence their future through the development of business relationships and contracting strategies. When these are done well, they have the capacity to control their markets. Now, the challenge for the large group is the fact that they require high maintenance. The more physicians you bring together, the more need there is for mutual respect, effective listening, and consensus building. When these qualities are present, the large group can maintain a powerful position in the marketplace. Some of these groups will be hospital owned or controlled, but many will be the traditional physician medical practice.

I am not suggesting that there is no place for the soloist or small group in the future. Depending on the environment, these individuals and units can be successful. But they will need to seek out and find their niches. And they will need to accept the fact that they will have consistent challenges in controlling their own destiny.

For those individuals who maintain a passion for their work, I would encourage them to continue on and be a part of one of the noblest professions in the world. For those who continually stress over the potent nature of the industry, I would suggest they look for a less stressful avocation in life, because the dynamic nature of the profession will only continue.

Mr. Bohlmann is a principal in the Medical Group Management Association Health Care Consulting Group in Denver, Colorado, and was president of the Medical Group Management Association in 1988.

Strategy

John T. Casey

WHEN I THINK of a strategic challenge during my career, the Presbyterian St. Luke's Health System in Denver and its sale in 1985 to a for-profit hospital management company comes to mind. Our organization, Presbyterian St. Luke's Health System, had actually undertaken a significant strategic planning effort a few years before the sale.

As a result of a merger, our system had two big hospitals (both around 500 beds) within blocks of one another in downtown Denver. We needed to do something about consolidating these hospitals, but this was during a time of intrusive certificate-of-need activity in regulatory oversight in Colorado. We proposed consolidating the hospitals by reducing beds by two or three hundred, then using those extra beds to build a satellite facility in another growing part of Denver. Our plan was turned down by the regulatory authority.

"Plan B" was to come up with another strategy we could mold into an acceptable proposal that we could sell politically. Demographics helped us identify where the hot growth areas were and how they matched with accessible providers of care and facilities. We came out with a very ambitious and attractive new plan that still called for the consolidation of the two hospitals downtown onto one site. We also proposed, however, to give up some net beds in order to build a very small hospital in one of the suburbs and, more importantly, the construction of an extensive array of upscale, large, sophisticated outpatient facilities in growing parts of the community.

Finally, we had a plan that we felt we could (and ultimately did) sell to the planning authorities, but it was going to require an extensive capital outlay to consolidate the two big hospitals and construct major outpatient facilities. We wanted full diagnostic capabilities and outpatient birthing—pretty state-of-the-art stuff at that time—and not just "doc in a box" facilities.

The dilemma our new plan created was that while we didn't have a significant amount of debt, we also didn't have a significant amount of cash. We were going to have to incur a substantial debt load to execute the strategic plan. We were very concerned about doing that in the face of the developing PPO movement and the HMO incursion into the market. All of a sudden we were seeing a very new trend of intense negotiation over price and seeing our rates hammered, particularly by the nongovernmental payers.

All this was creating pressure on the revenue side for us, and here we were proposing an expansive $240 million strategic plan. Contemplation of incurring that kind of debt in the face of increased prices, competitiveness, and intensity is what basically led us to make the strategic decision to seek out a partner. Our original plan had never considered the sale to a for-profit entity. We were trying to do what was right and what we felt we needed to do to maintain our competitiveness in the market place.

Our first thought was "Let's see if we can find a joint venture partner to come help carry some of this load with us, someone who has experience in the development of these kind of ambulatory facilities." We started talking to an outpatient surgery group that had spun out of Hospital Corporation of America (HCA). It was a process of dialogue and analysis that we nurtured carefully and professionally. We structured a very complete request for proposal.

First, for the joint venture partnership, we started looking at who might be a good partner to work with. For some of the ambulatory facilities, we were going to maintain ownership of the hospitals.

It was through this process early on that our eyes were opened.

Wesley in Wichita, Kansas, was just going through the process and deciding about sale. It was a very controversial event in the industry. We were one step behind them and so tried to take into account the criticisms that were leveled against them for how they went through that process of decision making and of the deal's structure itself. There were a lot of people who complained that they were buying themselves with their own money because of how their foundation had been structured. They were putting all this money into a nonprofit foundation that had many of the hospital's obligations to support.

We wanted to ensure that we avoided the trap of being susceptible to that sort of criticism and making it a true "arm's length sale." In fact, we put covenants and constraints into the deal to ensure that.

The biggest component of our plan was that we insisted, as part of a very legalistic approach to the contractual document itself, that the firm and specific commitments be made ultimately by American Medical International (AMI), who bought Presbyterian St. Luke's on the execution of the strategic plan. They basically set aside capital commitments for a several-year period to ensure that they would build out the ambulatory facilities, consolidate the hospitals, and the whole plan.

It was those legal constraints that caused them, several years later, to sell the hospitals back to the community when they got into trouble because they badly overspent on the hospital consolidation downtown. We had a $240 million budget, and they ended up spending considerably more than that amount. We had put them into the corner of having to follow through on those commitments and did not give them any wiggle room.

When AMI got in trouble later and had all those shareholder suits going, they didn't have the money to follow through on their commitments. They had no option but to sell it back. They really didn't want to, but the board of the foundation, which was legally responsible for overseeing the relationship with AMI, insisted that they follow through with the strategic plan. The board held their feet to the fire and they had to honor their commitments. All of this made it a very different sale and subsequent project than most of the outright "just changing hands" type of deals that later occurred between for-profits and not-for-profits.

Looking back, I think the strategy we created ended up being perfect. If you look at the ambulatory facilities that did get built, they are now the most successful in the Denver market.

Mr. Casey was the chairman and CEO of the Physician Reliance Network from 1997 to 1999.

Strategy

Maurice W. Elliott

ONE OF THE biggest strategic challenges of my career was an event that consisted of two phases: the process of acquiring a pediatric hospital, followed by the process of integrating it into, and merging its functions with, those of an adult healthcare system.

In the early 1990s, Le Bonheur Children's Medical Center, a 225-bed tertiary pediatric hospital located in the Memphis Medical Center, began thinking about long-term strategies to ensure financial viability in an increasingly competitive market.

In 1993, the president of Le Bonheur began talks with both my organization, Memphis Hospitals of Memphis, and Baptist Memorial. We were the two major adult healthcare providers in town, and Le Bonheur was exploring partnership arrangements with us whereby it would help us meet the needs of our pediatric patients so they could preserve their long-term financial viability in providing tertiary pediatric services. They were worried that the two major adult care systems in the area would develop competing pediatric services that would threaten their future. Le Bonheur's brainchild was for an agreement whereby both Baptist and Methodist would commit to using Le Bonheur for their respective pediatric services, in effect securing guaranteed financial support.

Baptist, which represented the greatest competitive threat to Le Bonheur, rejected Le Bonheur's proposal outright; instead, Baptist considered acquiring Le Bonheur. After lengthy negotiations, however,

Baptist decided it would be less costly to develop their own pediatric services.

Given the same proposal, Methodist Hospitals also became interested in the possibility of acquiring Le Bonheur. In analyzing the financial impact of the proposed acquisition, it was determined that if the Le Bonheur corporate entity was dissolved and instead licensed as a part of Methodist Hospitals of Memphis, significant increases in Medicare share and graduate medical education payments would be netted. These revenue enhancements, combined with other operating efficiencies, would result in a positive financial gain of more than $14 million during the first year.

There were several other advantages and benefits to acquiring Le Bonheur vs. another medical center:

- Le Bonheur's outstanding regional reputation and fiscal strength;
- Le Bonheur's provision of pediatric services would complement the quality of care throughout Methodist Hospitals of Memphis system, which had no pediatric service;
- because the University of Tennessee's pediatric residency program was UT's strongest and was housed at Le Bonheur, the relationship between the UT School of Medicine and Methodist would be strengthened, a long-time goal of Methodist; and
- the mission, culture, and management style of the two organizations were quite compatible.

After lengthy negotiations, Le Bonheur was acquired by Methodist on October 5, 1995. Since then, an effort has been made to maintain the separate identity of Le Bonheur. When patients are on Le Bonheur's campus, the Methodist name is not apparent. However, Methodist capitalized on the Le Bonheur name in all promotional materials, namely by the use of "Methodist–Le Bonheur Healthcare."

Since the acquisition, the former chief operating officer for Le Bonheur has been made a senior vice president for Methodist Healthcare with responsibilities for pediatric services throughout the system and ambulatory services in the Memphis market. Inpatient pediatric units have been developed at two of the Methodist hospitals that serve as referral facilities for seven other rural Methodist hospitals. These units are staffed and managed by Le Bonheur Children's Medical Center. While this has resulted in billing challenges and some management ambiguity, it ensures a continuity of high-quality pediatric care.

Methodist also continued to give all managed care programs equal access to Le Bonheur and equal pricing.

Methodist was careful to nurture the 600-strong volunteer corps of Le Bonheur. While all fundraising efforts are merged, funds raised by Le Bonheur are restricted for use by the pediatric hospital.

To fulfill the desires of both Methodist and Le Bonheur to make the result of the merger greater than the sum of its parts, a foundation was formed and a portion of its funds were used to create The Partnership for Women's and Children's Health. In collaboration with UT, several pilot projects have since measurably improved women's and children's health in the region.

Although the merging of the two organizations' cultures has occurred, which is not surprising as they were compatible to begin with, it has taken continuous work. The expected problems arose and have all needed to be dealt with: standardizing benefit programs, salary ranges, titles, materials management, information systems, and governance.

More recently, the medical staffs of the two institutions were merged as a result of the requirements of the Joint Commission on Accreditation of Healthcare Organizations.

The Le Bonheur board became an advisory board that reviews, approves, and makes recommendations to the Methodist Healthcare board on issues such as medical staff appointments, capital and operating budgets, and strategic plans.

To ensure a smooth transition, the agreement called for the Le Bonheur chief medical officer and former president to be ex-officio members of the Methodist Healthcare board of directors for a period of five years. These appointments have since continued beyond the five-year period.

What we have learned is that a merger like ours is not successful by accident, even when the cultures are compatible. It takes constant communication and sensitivity to the views and concerns of those in the organization being acquired. Problems and issues do arise and must be handled in a forthright manner and not be allowed to fester or be ignored.

Mr. Elliott is the president and CEO *of Methodist Healthcare in Memphis, Tennessee and was the chairman of the Tennessee Hospital Association from 1991 to 1992.*

Strategy

Earl J. Frederick

THE MOST IMPORTANT client of Children's Memorial Hospital in Chicago during my tenure was the State of Illinois. At the time, 55 percent of our inpatient and outpatient volume was Medicaid. To a varying degree, the dependence on Medicaid prevailed at some of the other children's hospitals in the state as well. Overall, the State of Illinois grossly underpaid the children's hospitals, and this was a problem.

Little relief was attainable through the efforts of the Illinois Hospital Association, as it was concerned with meeting the needs of all healthcare organizations, rather than addressing the needs of a specific hospital or strictly hospitals. A strategy was needed.

We addressed the problem by forming a coalition of children's hospitals serving Illinois Medicaid children and engaging a lobbyist, who worked with the CEOs of the hospitals as well as others from the hospitals' staffs (public relations, financial agents, physicians). Then we formed a strategy to educate the governor's staff and leadership in the legislative branch and their staffs on the unique needs of the children for whom they were responsible through the Medicaid program. We showed them the degree to which they were shortchanging the hospitals and physicians through financial analysis and enlightened them on what other states were doing.

Our approach was always focusing on the needs of children, not of the specific needs of the hospitals per se. Thus, it did not appear as though we were self-serving.

In effect, we were successful in increasing the state's appropriation for Medicaid. Thus, the total amount of money for Medicaid was increased by the amount we were able to convince the governor and legislators through negotiations was necessary to meet the needs of those children we served. Although we never realized our full costs, we received enough (with endowment monetary support) to break even on Medicaid patients.

The lesson I learned was that we could not solve a problem of this magnitude by ourselves—that is, Children's Memorial Hospital going it alone and pleading with the state that they were shortchanging Illinois children as well as our hospital.

Although the three children's hospitals in the metro Chicago area compete for specialty care as well as private patients, we were able to come together on a strategy on behalf of children, rather than individual hospitals, and collectively achieve success where we had each alone failed before.

If I faced the same situation today, I would use the same approach again. In fact, this process has now been used for ten years by the collection of children's hospitals in the metro Chicago area with continued success. It has led to a strong advocacy program on behalf of children in the state and now includes trustee involvement as well as medical staff leadership.

On a larger scale, we have also worked together with the staff of the National Association of Children's Hospitals and Related Institutions to educate the legislative and executive branches of the federal government. We've addressed elected officials and their staffs on the special needs of children. This effort has also been quite successful.

My advice to today's healthcare organization leaders:

- Accept that it may not always be possible to solve each problem you face from within your own organization.
- Remember that our institutions, for the most part, are not-for-profit and that it is better to have a strong commitment to service and meeting people's needs.

- Coming together on behalf of those we serve can successfully achieve hospitals' needs, even though we regularly compete among ourselves.
- Provide the leadership to your organization and those who work with you to successfully carry out your organization's mission.
- Provide the vision and direction to successfully accomplish your goals.

Mr. Frederick is the chairman of the board of advisors for Stockamp & Associates and was the president and CEO *of the Children's Memorial Hospital in Chicago, Illinois from 1980 to 1995.*

Strategy

Robert L. Goldstein, FACMPE

A NUMBER OF years ago, the chairman of the board of the Browne-McHardy Clinic in Metairie, Louisiana, and I began to recognize that dramatic changes were occurring in the local and national healthcare market. We wanted to remain competitive and viable and decided that the clinic needed to develop, pursue, and execute a strategy that would transcend short-term and mid-term timelines.

After much discussion and collaboration with clinic leadership, we made a strategic decision to focus on finding a capital and growth partner whose vision paralleled ours of being a physician-driven and -directed healthcare system. This physician-focused approach was adopted to propel our organization forward into expansion. This strategy of adding a large number of like-minded physicians and physician practices was seen as a win-win for the right partner and ourselves.

Over the next six-year period, the chairman and I began investigating numerous potential partners. During this time, serious discussions ensued with two strong suitors. The talks sometimes exceeded a year. Unfortunately, neither potential partner turned out to be optimal candidates.

Finally, after 24 months of negotiations with Christus Health, we were able to conclude an arrangement to create the Summit Health Group on February 1, 1999. The new company, equally owned by physicians and Christus Health, was designed to be a physician-driven, physician-integrated healthcare organization. Summit Health

Group was developed to prosper via physician operating divisions, or small operating units designed to protect and encourage local culture and direction under the administrative umbrella of Summit Health Group.

The process of creating Summit Health Group was arduous and dynamic. We worked hard and gained experience and knowledge in a wide variety of disciplines. Our skills as communicators and consensus builders were sharpened as we compiled and communicated information to our physician partners. As managers, we quickly needed to understand and synthesize a great deal of information from a number of disciplines such as finance, law, and organizational theory. This knowledge was necessary to develop the skill sets needed to deal with the new issues at hand. The need to balance the requirements of our then-current partner physicians with those of our new enterprise was an ever-present and underlying theme.

Upon reflection, we learned two valuable lessons.

First, the chairman and I should have recognized more quickly that our two earlier attempts were not going to bear fruit. We invested much more time and effort than we should have because we wanted those ventures to succeed. Consequently, we persisted when we really knew that we should move on. However, the experience of the two failed attempts did prove to be important learning tools for us as well as our physicians. The process established the foundation of knowledge necessary for our future modeling.

Second, the two-year timeline to establish Summit Health Group put a significant strain on the Browne-McHardy Clinic. The process of negotiation and deliberation siphoned off valuable focus and intensity from the group practice's daily operations and management.

In addition, several plans and strategies that we developed early in the process no longer made sense by the time the organization actually began operating. We have concluded that negotiations that last more than 12 months are probably more harmful than helpful to the venture.

Finally, I would suggest that the most important lesson we learned from this six-year adventure is that flexibility and agility are the key ingredients in managing a medical group enterprise successfully. One should be able to alter the course, to turn challenges into opportunities, and opportunities into successful initiatives. At the same time, management cannot lose sight of long-term goals that must be tied to maintaining the organization's core vision and values.

Mr. Goldstein is the CEO of Summit Health Group, L.L.C., in Metairie, Louisiana. He was board chair of the Medical Group Management Association in 2000 and president of the American College of Medical Practice Executives in 1994.

Strategy

Douglas D. Hawthorne, FACHE

Texas Health Resources (thr) and Baylor Health Care System (bhcs) attempted a merger that we believed would maximize the benefit both organizations provided to the community. The proposed name for the newly formed organization was Southwest Health System (shs), which was to contain an operations company called bhp Health Services (bhp). When we began the process, thr and bhcs established the following "Principles of Affiliation" to:

- Benefit the communities in the areas of improved quality, access, cost, and the preservation of choice.
- Maintain and enhance patient care, research, education, and community service.
- Recognize that key strategic decisions must be made based solely on the best interest of shs, bhp, and the affiliates as a whole.
- Provide for full integration of financial resources, governance, and management so that shs, bhp, and the affiliates function as a single economic unit.
- Advance delivery, financing, and management strategies, which will optimize attractiveness of the provider network, and enhance quality and the physician-patient relationship.
- Recognize shs/bhp's employees and related physicians as its most significant asset, enabling the pursuit of its mission and vision by providing a tremendous reservoir of knowledge and talent.

- Be subject to existing legal and other obligations of the member organizations.
- Include all other healthcare entities to align or affiliate with any founding sponsor and/or SHS.
- Enable the development and implementation of a market-based growth strategy in conjunction with physicians and regional partners.
- Operate in a manner that minimizes administrative and overhead costs.
- Preserve and enhance existing religious and church affiliations, mission, vision, values, heritage, name, and community-based nonprofit status.

We developed a formal negotiating process that involved board members, management, physicians, outside consultants, and outside legal counsel. As part of the process we developed a Transition Management Plan to guide an orderly integration and transition planning process between THR and BHCS. At the height of transition planning, 300 board members, physicians, and employees were involved through 60 transition planning councils. The purpose of the plan was to organize, direct, monitor, and track implementation of an orderly process for integrating customer-oriented, efficient, cost-effective services to support achievement of the SHS mission, vision, and principles of the affiliation. The plan was locally linked so that there was no disconnection from the hospitals or physicians. It was also developed with physician input and was managed with physicians. The process led to a strong conclusion to combine the two organizations and form SHS. However, after ten months of work, the boards of both organizations called off the transaction.

Through the process of attempting to merge, both organizations more clearly learned their own strengths and weaknesses. Both organizations came to understand the cultural differences in each other and learned the following lessons.

1. You must close the transition quickly
   - The longer it takes, the more likely it will not close.

- It is best to close the deal first and then move to integration planning afterwards.
- You must have decisive decision making.
- Consensus takes time—know when to say "when."
- Telltale trouble signs: missed deadlines and a lengthy process.

2. Clearly understand the negotiating process
   - Have negotiating teams from each side with similar levels of authority.

3. Use one set of consultants and attorneys
   - Try to use one set of consultants and attorneys to facilitate and help negotiate the transaction.

4. Have early agreement on governance structure
   - You must have early agreement on governance structure and how it will work. Clearly define roles and responsibilities of each board to know "where the buck stops."

5. In mergers, in terms of management, people are most important
   - Select the CEO first.
   - You must have timely decisions and actions regarding the selection of management.
   - You must answer questions early on about who to keep and who to let go at the senior management level.
   - Provide incentive to stabilize leadership and reward those who stay long term.

6. Informal due diligence process is essential
   - The better the informal process, the better the chance for the transaction to occur.

7. The intangibles (verbal/nonverbal) are essential to success
   - Commitment (the real "C" word)
   - Trust
   - Culture
   - Alignment

8. Strive for early wins
   - Don't just strive for early wins, celebrate them.

9. Communication is a critical key to success
   - Keep balance in content of message and parallel the depth of communication within the two organizations.

- To all stakeholders: the void of information will be filled with rumors, speculations, and worst case, intentionally inaccurate information.
- Maintain a good relationship with press, regulators, and public officials.
- Maintain timely, reliable, two-way communications throughout the organization.

10. Sometimes you need to call off a transaction
- It is not a failure to call off a transaction if there is a sense that things are not going right or market factors change.

My final advice to others is that it is critical to develop your board members and a significant group of physicians so they can provide timely input and participate in setting and/or approving strategies and tactics for the system and its individual units. This will require a focused effort on maintaining timely, reliable, two-way communications throughout the system so that all of the key stakeholders are on the same page and can work together toward achieving the mission and vision of the organization.

Mr. Hawthorne is the president and CEO of Texas Health Resources in Dallas, Texas and has been on the American Hospital Association board of trustees since 1998.

Strategy

Karen Ignagni

IN 1993, I left the American Federation of Labor–
Congress of Industrial Organizations (AFL-CIO) to join the Group
Health Association of America (GHAA) as its president. At a time
when managed care appeared to be on the verge of becoming the
predominant form of healthcare delivery in the United States, the
selection committee believed that my professional experience could
contribute to an industry that would help shape the future.

In consultation with the board of directors, I came to GHAA with a
list of three initial priorities:

1. to develop a first-class lobbying organization for the health plan
    industry;
2. to create a strong healthcare policy and research shop; and
3. to recruit experienced staff and build an effective team to carry out
    GHAA's development plan.

During reorganization, we realized that the nature of lobbying Congress in Washington, DC was changing rapidly. The process had gone
from being an inside game to one that was now squarely in the sunlight
of public scrutiny. The future of GHAA depended on adapting to this
changing environment and using it to best represent our member
companies. Accordingly, we began to look for new models to guide us
into the twenty-first century. To actively compete in this new world, we
knew the key lay in having the best available healthcare information
and analysis, along with the ability to speak with one voice for the

entire managed care community. To accomplish this, GHAA merged with the American Managed Care and Review Association (AMCRA) in 1996. The new entity, the American Association of Health Plans (AAHP), could now speak on behalf of the entire managed care industry and deliver a clear message on behalf of HMOs, PPOs, and other similar health plans.

AAHP has employed a very proactive approach in interacting with Capitol Hill and other constituents in the healthcare arena. Instead of being reactive, we set out to create an offensive strategy.

We regularly reach out to Congress to offer our insight, research, or technical assistance regarding various healthcare issues. We also gather data for and about our member plans, which can then be used in improving the delivery of care, managing resources, and controlling costs. We also help provide various patient-centered information programs that enable the public to better understand managed care and help health plan participants learn how to improve their quality of life by using their plans more effectively.

AAHP's total membership has tripled over the past seven years to now include more than 1,000 plans that provide healthcare coverage to more than 140 million Americans. Today, AAHP is a member-directed organization focused on responding to the concerns of patients and providers. We continue to have a proactive, well-defined strategy that allows for flexibility in adjusting to the constantly changing environment around us. We have emerged as one of the leading voices in healthcare policy, research, and advocacy by providing reliable, meaningful information to healthcare decision makers and to the public at large.

As we step into the twenty-first century, AAHP as an organization has also learned important lessons along the way that have since made our work extend beyond the bounds of Capitol Hill:

- plans didn't realize all of the implications of an industry in transition, and they were initially caught off guard by the tidal wave of opposition to managed care from provider groups;
- our industry underestimated the need to foster two-way communication with consumers during the rapid transition to managed care; and

- we didn't commit resources to describing the value of managed care to the American people.

These lessons gave rise to the industry's *Code of Conduct*, administrative simplification efforts to reduce the paperwork burdens on doctors, proposals for reducing the number of uninsured in America, as well efforts to establish voluntary ombudsman programs and processes for the independent review of medical decisions. We have also released principles on improving patient safety and favor reform of the Medicare system to preserve it for future generations and provide prescription drugs to seniors while making sure that they continue to have the safety net of choice within the system. AAHP also continues to support highly successful disease management programs and collaborations with the various disease groups, such as the American Diabetes Association, to improve the quality of healthcare delivered to patients in the managed care system.

As we look ahead, it is increasingly important for health plan leaders and medical directors to be out front and tell their stories about what their organizations are doing to promote better healthcare. In today's information-driven age, it is critical that we continue to define who and what we are as a maturing industry.

My experience with the AAHP has taught me three important lessons:

- Success comes from clearly articulating the goals of your organization and then working toward them.
- Leaders of lobby organizations must constantly assess the environment facing and surrounding the industry they represent and be flexible enough to change strategies or tactics when necessary.
- Most importantly, companies in the healthcare delivery field must listen to what their customers and partners are telling them and work to be responsive to these needs.

Ms. Ignagni is president and CEO of the American Association of Health Plans in Washington, DC.

Strategy

L. R. (Rush) Jordan, LFACHE

DURING MY CAREER as chief executive officer at Miami Valley Hospital in Dayton, Ohio in the early 1980s, our organization encountered a strategic challenge to improve our emergency ambulance service, which was having problems transporting injured patients during traffic jams.

Our medical center was located in a city of one million citizens. At the north, south, east, and west of the metro area, interstates crisscrossed the city. Although the city was highly industrialized, it was surrounded by farmland.

Our medical center had invested heavily in developing the region's top ER/trauma center. Farm accidents, industrial accidents, and interstate accidents were frequent occurrences. Many times, the traffic congestion resulting from interstate accidents delayed our ambulances from reaching the injured in a timely fashion. This problem was serious—lives were at stake.

Management, the board, and emergency/trauma physicians met, and all data indicated our city needed an air ambulance service. Other cities in the region with air ambulance services were visited and their services were studied. We decided to develop a business plan for our own service.

When the business plan was finished and approved by the emergency/trauma physicians, it was presented to the board. The business plan indicated the service would have to be subsidized for a minimum of two years. The board instructed management to seek the cooperation of the other four general acute care hospitals and the Children's Medical Center in establishing a citywide company with landing sites at all six hospitals.

When I called the local CEOs from the other hospitals, I got a lukewarm response. We proposed holding seminars on the topic with the aid of a consultant and another organization that had such a service to stimulate further discussion. Although they seemed interested in the idea, they would not agree to help pay for the seminars. We decided to finance the seminars ourselves. The CEOs all attended and brought along members of their medical staff, management staff, and board of trustees.

The seminars seemed successful, as lively discussions ensued.

When the CEOs went back to their organizations and asked their medical staffs and boards to decide, however, they all declined participation. Not only did they not want to be partners with us in this venture but they also rejected our suggestion that they build landing sites at their facilities. Their concerns appeared to be more rooted in competition than cooperation. However, since the agreement proposed that every hospital would have equal ownership shares and would have equal representation on the community board, the most probable explanation for their rejection was the perception that it was too risky to invest the finances.

The news of the other hospitals' unanimous rejections was given to our medical staff executive committee, who didn't hesitate to move ahead with the project. They unanimously recommended to our board that we proceed with the development of the air ambulance service on our own.

After months of detailed planning, recruiting, and training of personnel, along with construction, we were ready. Our medical center announced the opening of our air ambulance service, which we dubbed "Care Flight."

Morale and enthusiasm were high throughout our organization after the launch of the new service. We were getting the critically injured to medical emergency care faster than a ground ambulance could, and we were feeling heroic. Seconds count in lifesaving.

Print and broadcast media gave our new service outstanding coverage. Within a few weeks, Care Flight was a regular feature on the evening news whenever serious local accidents were reported. Helicopters provide dramatic television footage, and our name was on that helicopter.

Special orientation sessions were held for all emergency ambulance technicians in the area with excellent results. Each month we recorded an increase in flights resulting in our medical center becoming the region's leader in trauma care.

After 14 months, the air ambulance began operating at a slight profit. The excellent coverage by the media continued to be a public relations bonanza for our organization.

At the end of two years, one by one, the other hospitals and centers in the region who had declined participation started contacting us. They all said they now wanted to construct helicopter pads for day and night landing and wanted us to consider them as landing sites. They wanted us to bring them patients with our air ambulance helicopter service. Although they didn't want a business partnership in the operation, just to contract with our service, this time we could have been the ones to turn them down. Our medical staff and board decided we should cooperate. I am a firm believer that healthcare is a local community service and that every effort should be made to develop cooperative services whenever possible. If, however, sincere efforts to promote cooperation fail, your organization must proceed to provide a needed service to the citizens of your community.

Although they didn't want to partner with us, they also did not want us to be taking their patients to our hospital. They told us if we'd commit to delivering their patients to their hospitals, they would build landing sites. Our board decided to go ahead with it because giving patients and their families a choice as to where they wanted to be taken was best for patients. In any event, we had already established our reputation in the emergency and trauma arena. An overwhelming majority of patients knew about Miami Valley's helicopter or saw the name on the helicopter and said, "I want to go to Miami Valley."

If I had to give a piece of advice to other healthcare professionals it would be to make a first-class, good-faith effort to provide the services your community needs. If you are not able to get cooperation from others, go ahead on your own—even if it's difficult—as long as it is financially feasible. The other would-be partners in the community may not be happy that you are taking the lead and striking out with an initiative on your own, but they had a choice.

Mr. Jordan is a professor of health administration at the University of Alabama at Birmingham and was the president of the Alabama Hospital Assocation in 1998.

Strategy

Gary A. Mecklenburg, CHE

IN A COMPLICATED, fast-changing world, the need for thoughtful planning and careful allocation of healthcare resources never has been greater. How can a successful CEO communicate and motivate a diverse set of employees, physicians, and constituents to fulfill the strategic direction of a complex hospital or healthcare system? A clearly stated, understood, and actualized sense of mission can be a powerful tool for achieving success.

In 1980, I became the president and CEO of St. Joseph's Hospital in Milwaukee, Wisconsin, the state's largest Catholic hospital. At that time, St. Joseph's was a successful hospital with a strong reputation and a hundred-year tradition of patient care, but an increasingly competitive marketplace and a changing financial environment were forcing the organization to reevaluate its direction and operations.

I had found true strategic planning to be difficult in the complicated, multipurpose, and highly political world of academic medical centers. Could a community-based teaching hospital sustain a classic approach to planning? A major consulting firm helped the administrative team assess and analyze the hospital's strengths and weaknesses, and this led to an outline of goals, objectives, strategies, and tactics, all of which needed to be measurable and time specific. However, any good strategic plan must begin with a clear statement of mission, the fundamental reason for an organization's existence that should guide the plan's direction.

The mission of the Wheaton Franciscan Sisters, who sponsor and own St. Joseph's Hospital, was "to fulfill the healing mission of Jesus Christ." For them, "healing" had implications beyond hospital services, encompassing the relationships between the hospital and its community and the hospital and its staff. While such a broad mission was acceptable for a religious congregation, it was a challenge to translate the healing philosophy into goals dealing with program development, physician recruitment, and financial performance. The hospital's mission didn't have to be identical to the Sisters', but it needed to be consistent.

As I became more familiar with the organization, I realized that the religious purpose of St. Joseph's Hospital was a great motivator and the underlying reason why many of our physicians and employees chose to work there. For many employees, their role at St. Joseph's was not just a job, but daily fulfillment of their beliefs and values.

For example, I remember Emma, the housekeeper responsible for cleaning the main lobby where a large statue of St. Joseph stood to welcome visitors. As I got to know Emma, I realized that salary was incidental to her real job: fulfilling the responsibilities of her faith. It wasn't the hospital's lobby—it was God's lobby, and Emma kept it spotlessly clean for Him.

Over time, I learned that a large number of our staff, whether Catholic or not, worked harder and longer, volunteered for many activities, and came in on weekends and holidays because they fundamentally believed in the importance of the organization's work and their personal role within it. Translation of the Sisters' mission into strategies, decision making, and resource allocation became clear. Simply stated, if we did "the right thing" for our patients and the community, business success would follow.

After five years, the hospital successfully completed its strategic plan and was strong, as measured by volume, financial performance, and community relations. With a clear sense of the value of strategic planning and of the importance of mission, I left St. Joseph's in 1985 and returned to the world of academic medical centers at Northwestern

Memorial Hospital (NMH) in Chicago. I had learned that with good planning and execution, you could "move" an organization toward fulfilling its purpose. It was not clear, however, whether one could achieve similar results in a larger organization that did not have the benefit of religious sponsorship.

As we worked on our first strategic plan at NMH, we spent days defining the essential mission of the hospital. A new chair of surgery observed that " . . . even though Northwestern Memorial Hospital is an academic medical center, the patient always comes first." This became the first line of a restated mission that explained the essential relationship underlying high quality patient service and academic excellence. Finally, we had a core motto: "Patients First." Many watched to see if the new management team really would make decisions primarily based on what is best for patients. Was this just politically correct rhetoric?

As we allocated capital to improve service, enhanced staffing, and celebrated higher patient satisfaction scores, administrative credibility increased. Executive compensation was based on team goals to achieve the strategy and improve quality, and a performance-based bonus program was extended to every employee, encouraging organization-wide continuous improvement. We sought leaders with a patient focus, and nurse managers were promoted to fill senior management positions, from COO to vice president of support services. Enthusiasm and commitment increased across the institution.

Performance rose consistently, as measured by higher volume, lower costs, and improved financial results. In a city filled with well-known academic medical centers, the hospital was ranked as the one having the best nurses, doctors, and services, making it the "most preferred" in Chicago.

When the organization committed to an ambitious replacement of all inpatient and outpatient facilities, requiring almost ten years of planning and construction, "Patients First" was again tested. Could a two-million-square-foot building housing 500 beds and 500 physician practices combine a warm, caring, patient-focused environment with a high-tech center supporting teaching and clinical research? Would window walls with spectacular views of the city and Lake Michigan go to patients and visitors, or would offices for executives and physicians receive top priority?

It was important that physicians shared in the design of a "Patients First" environment. Working with the dean of the medical school, we developed several pages of guidelines for the architects and planners. We agreed that if we reached a point where we had to choose between physician convenience and what was best for the patient, the decision clearly would be made for the patient. At first, the architects questioned our commitment, but after several revisions of their early work, they knew we were serious.

Thus, the entire front of the building, with all its windows and light, was dedicated to waiting space, lounges for patients and families, and to public elevators, a design that makes it easier for people to remain oriented in a large, complicated facility.

Since it opened on May 1, 1999, the new Northwestern Memorial Hospital has been an enormous success, hailed by patients, clinicians, architects, and planners around the world for its innovative design and comfortable environment. "It doesn't look like a hospital" is the most common reaction. From the art on the walls to the large private rooms with an extra bed for a family member to spend the night, the facility responds to patients and families.

After the first year of operation in a declining market, inpatient volume grew more than 15 percent, with visits to ancillary services and doctors offices up even more. With nursing and workforce shortages a major problem across the country, turnover and vacancy rates at NMH are down, and the use of "agency" nurses has been virtually eliminated. The quality of candidates for physician leadership positions is significantly better. The organization is financially sound, one of only four in the nation to hold an AA+ credit rating. Medical staff and employees exude a confidence and enthusiasm that is rare in healthcare today. Everyone in the organization believes that the consistent focus on quality and patient service is a unifying factor. "Patients First" has improved every dimension of the academic medical center.

In 20 years as a hospital CEO, I've learned that a team of people committed to a common vision can accomplish great things. There is strength in mission if it provides a consistent framework for decision making and allocation of resources. Finally, a common sense of purpose, whether religious or secular, can be a powerful motivational force for even the largest and most complicated organizations.

Mr. Mecklenburg is the president and CEO of Northwestern Memorial Hospital in Chicago, Illinois and chairman of the American Hospital Association for 2001.

Strategy

Joseph W. Mitlyng, Jr., FACMPE

I CAME TO Park Nicollet Medical Center as executive vice president and chief operating officer in March of 1986. I was brought into a turnaround situation. The previous leadership had left or had been voted out of office in January. Park Nicollet Clinic had lost $2 to $3 million dollars in each of the previous three years, and was down to its last $3 million of net worth.

Although it started out as a dire situation when I came aboard, we managed to slowly rebuild our assets. Over eight years, from 1986 to 1994, net worth increased from $3 million to $36 million. Physician and staff compensation became competitive, and we renovated or replaced facilities and equipment.

When I was hired the situation was grim. The physicians had been subjected to significant salary withholds in the prior two years, which had yet to be paid. Their incomes were between the 20th and the 50th percentile nationally for their specialties. A wage and hiring freeze was enacted the year before. Staff turnover was 36 percent. To start with, I needed to determine why we were losing money.

People were working hard. During my first year, an ambulatory care accreditation surveyor commented on how hard people were working. He said, "In most places, the receptionists look up and smile when I come into the waiting room. Your people have their heads down, one hand holding the phone to their head, and with the other hand they are writing as fast as they can." This made me understand that our staff was not to blame, so I began assessing Park Nicollet in other areas.

46

Park Nicollet had a global capitation risk (physician, hospital, and pharmacy costs) for 165,000 patients, or 65 percent of its practice. Park Nicollet also had significant assets that were not reflected on the balance sheet: it had a 20 percent market share in Minneapolis and had a 14-location satellite network that covered Minneapolis and most of its suburbs. It had a 60 percent ownership in MedCenters Health Plan, a company formed to manage the HMO that Park Nicollet had founded in 1972.

Despite all these assets, we were still losing money. The seriousness of the situation was underscored at my first meeting with someone outside of the organization. I was only two weeks on the job when I had lunch with our banker. After a few minutes of pleasantries, the banker looked at me and asked: "Should we call your note?" The note was for $650,000. The repayment terms were $50,000 per year, and we were current with our payments. Apparently, because of our declining financial health, our ability to continue with our repayment was perceived to be questionable. I realized we had to determine the fundamental causes of the ongoing operating losses before we could create a strategy to turn the situation around.

It turned out that the primary cause of our losses was a shift in leadership emphasis to the profitability of our HMO company, Med-Centers Health Plan, at the expense of Park Nicollet, which provided its asset base.

Previous leadership wanted to capitalize on the income potential of the HMO. Because the HMO had to be not-for-profit in Minnesota, a for-profit management company was established with the idea of creating an earnings stream from administrative charges on premiums, in addition to a public stock offering.

Under the former leadership, the HMO had continued to price its products using the same strategy that had proved successful histori-cally: underpricing the competition. Underpricing worked well until the early 1980s when the HMOs were less than 25 percent of the market. By the mid-1980s, HMOs made up a bigger part of the market. The HMOs were now seeing each other as their primary competition, and they tried to underprice each other. Much like an old-fashioned corner gas station "price war," they underpriced each other right down below costs.

This is when our HMO, and thus Park Nicollet, started experiencing losses. Soon after I was hired I learned from the marketing director for the HMO that the price increase for the year was set to be 0.6 percent. When I asked him how he came up with that number, he said: "You don't know how tough things are out there. People want to pay less, they don't want to pay more." I later commented on how good his staff had become at selling "$5,000 Cadillacs."

To raise cash for Park Nicollet's operations, when our contract was up for renewal with MedCenters, we first sought to hold costs down. We negotiated terms in the new contract that said that they could not pay us less than our costs without our prior approval. Then we sold our 60 percent interest in MedCenters for $5.5 million in cash and contingent payments of $10.7 million that were recognized as revenues through 1994.

We had increased our assets but needed to better understand where we were losing money. In May 1987, our new chief financial officer conducted a "line of business" analysis. It was not a complex analysis, a ratio of costs to charges, but it provided the insight we needed. Two of our three businesses were producing strong profits—our fee-for-service practice and our retail division. Our third business, the capitated practice, was producing an annual operating loss of $10 million.

In August 1987, we informed MedCenters Health Plan that we needed a 13 percent increase to break even. They declined. We started arbitration in September, and by December 1987, we had an arbitration judgment in our favor for a $6 million capitation increase. That ignited a two-year litigation of *Park Nicollet v. MedCenters Health Plan* and appeals. We lost $2 million on global risk capitation for 12,000 seniors in 1987. It appeared that we needed to increase premiums to pay for our costs. The seniors' monthly premium for MedCenters Health Plan was $24.00. One competitor, SHARE, had the largest senior enrollment and had a premium of about $18.00. Another competitor, Physicians Health Plan (PHP, the beginnings of United Health Care), had a premium of about $23.00. The decision on the size of the senior premium increase had to be made by early November to meet the timing requirements for the Health Care Financing Administration (HCFA) review and notification of enrollees.

We decided to go with an increase of 50 percent to a premium of $36.00. The president and CEO of our hospital partner, Methodist Hospital, asked the tough question: "What if these seniors choose to leave?"

PHP had announced an increase of about 10 percent the week prior to our announcement. When they saw the size of our increase, they immediately rescinded their announcement of the previous week and announced a new increase, just below ours. Over the twelve months of 1988, we lost only six of the 12,000 enrollees (three died and two moved away).

In 1989 the litigation was finally decided in Park Nicollet's favor. The final decision was anticlimactic, however. The relationship between MedCenters and Park Nicollet had fundamentally changed. Capitation and pricing implications had become topics we discussed and planned together.

What we learned or reaffirmed:

- If revenue is not adequate, you cannot make it up by cutting expenses.
- If you are managing well and are bleeding red ink, your competitors are bleeding also.
- If your competitors are bleeding, they will follow a price increase.
- People pay more for perceived quality.
- At Park Nicollet Medical Center, the physicians' practice is the core business.

Park Nicollet and Methodist Hospital merged to form Health System Minnesota in 1994. Because Park Nicollet Clinic still has the strongest name recognition in Minneapolis, Health System Minnesota has announced it will be dropping that name and will now be known as Park Nicollet Health Services.

Mr. Mitlyng is a principal with Larson, Allen, Weishair & Co., L.L.P., in Orefield, Pennsylvania and was president of the Medical Group Management Association in 1994.

Strategy

Robert A. Nelson, FACMPE

WHILE MISSION STATEMENTS abound today, they were a rarity in the early 1970s in group medical practice. It wasn't until the 1980s that mission statements came into vogue in the healthcare industry.

In the 1970s, little thought was given to the long-term purpose of the healthcare organization. We simply went about the business of treating patients and generating a livable wage for physicians and staff. Little did we realize how much a written purpose or "mission statement" would change the Friendly Hills Medical Group when we convened our first serious medical staff retreat in the summer of 1976. The group was then composed of 12 physicians, mostly in family practice, and had only been in existence for a few years. The reason for the meeting was to discuss the logistics of daily operations and consider the advisability of entering into a prepaid contract with Blue Cross of California. What happened at that meeting changed the course of the group forever.

During our discussions, we continually found ourselves asking three key questions:

1. Why are we here?
2. What do we want to be?
3. Where are we going?

These questions understandably generated much debate and a variety of opinions. It became apparent that the only way to satisfactorily answer them was to produce a statement of purpose. Eventually, we produced a 17-word mission statement that set our direction for the next quarter of a century. That statement said, "Our mission is to deliver comprehensive, quality healthcare to our patients in a spirit of personal caring." For many years it was printed on the bottom of our stationery.

We also realized that one word from that statement would ultimately define our growth strategy. The word "comprehensive" suggested that we must be willing to offer a full range of services to patients. That meant transitioning from a primary care practice to a multispecialty group. Also implicit in the word "comprehensive" was a commitment to be on the leading edge of healthcare delivery.

We concluded at the retreat that prepaid medicine was going to be a major factor in healthcare delivery in the future. Accordingly, if we were going to be a leader in the medical community, we decided we should sign the Blue Cross contract and begin learning how to master the process. We clearly understood that when we signed the contract, we would be responsible for all physician services. This required us to establish a physician network.

We subsequently met with many of the specialists to whom we routinely referred patients, and others who expressed an interest in participating with us. In some cases, it was an easy sell. In other cases, physicians refused to cooperate. It didn't take long, however, for the naysayers to change their minds when we excluded them from our referral base.

These commitments to provide comprehensive services and to enter the world of prepaid care fueled our growth for the next 20 years.

We grew from five physicians in 1970 to roughly 80 physicians in 1986 when I left the group. Over time, many of the specialists in our extended network actually joined the staff of the Friendly Hills Medical Group. Ultimately, with more practice acquisitions, mergers, and the affiliation with CareMark, the practice mushroomed to 400 providers in the mid-1990s.

What did I learn about strategy from the Friendly Hills Medical Group experience? Several things:

- First, a mission statement is a vital part of any organization, not just window dressing in the lobby of the building. As a realistic, practical guide for the organization, it should provide a focus for the medical staff that is constantly reinforced through the years.
- Second, constant communication between the group's leadership and the medical staff is needed to keep the commitment strong. At Friendly Hills, we had medical staff meetings monthly to ensure that everyone was informed. Also, in the early years, two physicians shared an office with a partner's desk. This facilitated communication and kept individuals from feeling isolated. Later, as the practice grew, we could no longer do this, and it showed.
- Third, an intrepid leadership team is needed to keep the group focused on the mission. This includes a mutually respectful partnership of physicians and management.
- Fourth, having leverage is vital to accomplishing difficult tasks. Leverage does not come without a strong commitment and willingness to take calculated risks.

Finally, it occurs to me that there are many moderately successful medical groups operating in the country today, but very few really thriving ones. The difference is the effectiveness of leadership. The top organizations have strong, focused leaders who are trusted and respected by their medical and support staffs. The "so-so" groups have weak leadership with too much democracy and too much second-guessing to make the tough decisions necessary to excel.

Mr. Nelson is a principal with The Canon Group, L.L.C., in Santa Barbara, California. He was board chair of the American College of Medical Practice Executives in 2000 and president of the Medical Group Management Association in 1993.

Strategy

Stanley R. Nelson, LFACHE

IN MY CAREER as chief executive officer at Henry Ford Health System in Detroit during the early 1970s, I was challenged to find a solution to a big problem. Our healthcare system, which had a market of 4.5 million spread across southeast Michigan, was rapidly losing much of its patient base and medical talent. The situation seemed irreversible. We were destined to face dire consequences if something wasn't done fast.

To give you some background, go back in time to the 1950s, when tens of thousands of citizens of Detroit began moving to the suburbs. After the riots and civil disturbances of 1967, the exodus intensified. By the time the Henry Ford Health System started up in the center of the city in 1971, Detroit and its suburbs constituted one of the most polarized metropolitan areas in the country. Physicians and other healthcare providers followed the population migration, as did entire hospital organizations.

The demographic upheaval resulted in a significant number of loyal patients of Henry Ford Hospital seeking healthcare elsewhere (typically the suburbs). There was a strong conviction that unless Henry Ford Hospital could access its entire market, erosion of its patient base would continue with serious consequences. This situation prompted the leaders of our urban hospital to examine our options.

One option was to heed the conventional wisdom of the time and follow the "center of excellence" strategy—build excellence and the patients will come.

Another option was to build inpatient services by adding hospitals in the economically strong suburbs. However, this was not possible due to certificate-of-need constraints and an adequate supply of beds supplied by other healthcare providers.

A third option was chosen. It involved creating an ambulatory care strategy that would provide accessible, convenient, user-friendly, outpatient healthcare services to the suburbs. The goal of the strategy was to provide a Henry Ford healthcare access point within a 12 to 15 mile drive for 90 percent of Henry Ford's market population.

The initial steps included building facilities and designing programs for two major ambulatory care centers (75,000 square feet, which were subsequently doubled and tripled in size) located in the suburbs of Dearborn and West Bloomfield. These centers opened in 1975 and provided a wide range of services, including primary and specialty medical care, outpatient surgery, 24-hour emergency care, laboratory, radiology, pharmacy, physical therapy, and renal dialysis services. Early on, rotating physicians from the main hospital and clinic to the satellite centers on an as-needed basis provided subspecialty clinical services. As patient volumes increased, many of these subspecialty services were provided on a full-time basis.

Our strategy was working.

The new major care centers thrived and immediately began to expand the scope of their services and the extent of their clinical specialization. Additional centers varying in size and range of clinical services followed. By 1980, more than 30 such centers existed, permitting a regionalization of centers wherein referrals from primary or secondary care centers could be made to the major ambulatory care centers or, ultimately, to the main clinic and hospital in Detroit.

An early lesson learned was that accessibility, convenient parking, and user-friendly facilities were critically important. Many patients who had stopped going to the main clinic and hospital in Detroit several years earlier were now returning to the Henry Ford system because of the availability of the suburban centers.

And this was just the beginning.

With the continued growth and success of our ambulatory care system, the notion of adding a financing component to the system was explored. A feasibility study by the consulting staff from Kaiser-Permanente indicated that an HMO might succeed. The lack of population growth, however, and high penetration by Michigan Blue Cross Blue Shield were definite negatives.

In 1979, with the support and cooperation of United Auto Workers and the Ford Motor Company, the Health Alliance Plan (an HMO) was formed. Almost immediately, a remarkable synergy between the health plan and the ambulatory care system occurred. Each grew much more rapidly because of the other. It was now possible to cross-market each entity to the benefit of the total enterprise. Compounded growth rates of 18 to 20 percent were experienced for several years in a mature market with no population growth. By the end of 1988, the Health Alliance Plan members had reached 400,000 and in 1997 exceeded 500,000.

From this experience, we learned the following lessons.

- Think and plan in nontraditional ways (at the time our ambulatory care strategy was enacted, it was not generally accepted by hospitals).
- Organizational consensus is needed on the definition of your market.
- Define your business(es), understanding that each may require different management experience and skills.
- Use market research on an ongoing basis for its essential value in identifying the shifting needs and desires of your changing market and its subsets.
- Scale and balance are important when integrating health services; the various functional components of the system must be of adequate size and balance to make a synergistic contribution to the whole.

It's been said that "hindsight is 20–20"; if we could go back in time we might have been even more aggressive in deploying ambulatory care centers. We missed one if not more opportunities to build facilities in shopping centers. Today we see the value of placing a major ambulatory care facility at or near major regional suburban shopping centers.

My advice, then, to today's healthcare leaders is:

- understand what business(es) you are in;
- define and understand your market and its submarkets and that they constantly change;
- success in any endeavor is dependent on execution even more than strategy or tactics; and
- proper execution requires the right people, which means that management team selection and their professional development, growth, and coaching represent the most important contributions a CEO can make to his or her organization.

Mr. Nelson is the chairman of the Scottsdale Institute in Scottsdale, Arizona, and was president and CEO of Henry Ford Health Care Corporation in Detroit, Michigan, from 1976 to 1988.

Strategy

Margaret E. O'Kane

THE NATIONAL COMMITTEE for Quality Assurance (NCQA) is a private, nonprofit organization dedicated to improving the quality of our nation's healthcare. Its primary responsibilities are to assess and report on the quality of managed care plans. The information we gather is used by purchasers and consumers of care to distinguish between plans for the purpose of aiding them in making more informed healthcare purchasing decisions.

There was an early attempt at developing this kind of agency in 1979, but it ultimately failed in 1983 because there was no consistent demand for accountability in healthcare. I became the administrative leader for the NCQA when the entity was reconstituted and its modern era began in 1990.

My initial tasks were to furnish an office and create a small infrastructure to support the activities of the organization. Once that was done, we moved on to the real purpose of the agency: to figure out a way to move healthcare quality forward. We chose the managed care venue because we thought that large health plans were the most reasonable vehicle for integrating care.

Our first major challenge was to take a diverse set of stakeholders—physicians, HMO executives, government, and purchasers—and put them together in a model that would allow us to define quality. These stakeholders, along with consumer and labor representatives, quality experts, and policymakers, became our board of directors.

Our first realization was that each constituent had a different definition of quality, and each was convinced that his view was the correct one.

We spent the majority of 1990 and 1991 in developing standards and measures in five or six specific operational areas, then we embarked on a campaign to enroll managed care organizations in our rigorous, but voluntary, accreditation program.

The first watershed event occurred in 1991 when the Xerox Corporation announced that it would only execute managed care contracts with NCQA-accredited HMOs. Other significant employers began to follow soon after.

The second landmark event happened in 1993 when we successfully enticed some health plans into participating in our Health Plan Employer Data and Information Set (HEDIS) Report Card Pilot Project. HEDIS rocketed us into the public consciousness because it was designed to actually measure the health plan's performance by using a set of standardized measures. Where accreditation is the assessment of the quality of systems and processes that make up the health plan, HEDIS evaluates the results of performance in many key areas of care such as rates of immunizations, mammograms, and pap smears; diabetes and heart disease management; and member satisfaction.

We believe that we have now completed the first of three stages of organizational development by securing a meaningful relationship with managed care organizations. The next stage of our development plan includes the extension of the accreditation process to group medical practice, and an evolution to a more flexible, modular approach to accreditation that can be adapted to different types of organizations. The goal of stage three is to expand and extend our accreditation and outcomes programs to the remaining sectors of healthcare delivery. We don't have a firm timetable for completing this plan, but it seems likely to take another decade to accomplish these goals, given the volatility of the healthcare environment.

As you can imagine, the past decade was a mixture of organizational successes and failures. We are proud of the programs that we have introduced because they represent positive steps toward our ultimate goal of improving healthcare delivery in our country. We have, however, seen a significant public backlash against managed care, fueled by extensive anecdotal reporting by the media. This has forced some retrenchment, slowing down needed progress in reforming healthcare.

The other major roadblock to our progress has been the inability to gain consensus on defining quality. Until we're able to arrive at some universally acceptable definition of quality, it will limit our effectiveness in assessing and measuring the quality of care being delivered in America.

Of course, it's always instructive to look back at events of the past and analyze what could have been improved. As I look at the past decade of the NCQA, this is what I believe we could have done better:

- We should have begun the process of information dissemination to the public sooner than we did.
- We could have encouraged better relationship building between patients and HMOs.
- We should have pushed for better customer satisfaction measurement sooner.
- We should have realized earlier that each health plan is different and related to each accordingly.
- We could have put more emphasis on HMO customer service and communication.
- We could have done a better job of communicating to the public the idea that managed care can be a good vehicle for ensuring enhanced quality and service at a reasonable price.

Far from being discouraged by contemplation of this list, NCQA intends to use it to make us far more effective in the future.

The three most important lessons I have learned over the past ten years of moving the quality agenda forward are as follows:

1. Trying to solve a complex problem takes time; progress occurs in small increments, not in big leaps.
2. Constantly challenge your own paradigm and be willing to change your thought processes when necessary.
3. Victory is rarely complete; as a result, leaders must learn to celebrate partial victories along the way.

Ms. O'Kane is president of the National Committee for Quality Assurance in Washington, DC.

Strategy

Dennis S. O'Leary, M.D., HFACHE

"The mission of the Joint Commission on Accreditation of Healthcare Organizations is to continuously improve the safety and quality of care provided to the public through the provision of healthcare accreditation and related services that support performance improvement in healthcare organizations."

THERE IS NO question that the most compelling issue we face today is the management of medical errors in healthcare organizations. While most accredited organizations are continually in substantial compliance with the Joint Commission on Accreditation of Healthcare Organization's standards, it is disquieting that we still have an average of 10 to 12 medical disasters per hospital per year in the United States. That translates into death or permanent loss of bodily function for over 50,000 Americans annually.

The Joint Commission began intensive work in trying to reduce medical errors in healthcare organizations in 1995, and through the past five years it has debated and continuously refined its approach to the problem. Our initial reaction was, when we learned of a serious adverse event in an accredited organization, to punish the organization through reduction or revocation of its accreditation status. This approach was soon codified into the first iteration of our Sentinel Event Policy. However, sanctioning these organizations labeled them as "bad hospitals" in the eyes of the public, even though many of them were actually outstanding institutions. Once we recognized these flaws, we moved quickly to revise our approach.

Our second iteration of the Sentinel Event Policy took a more tempered approach and simply designated organizations that had experienced a serious adverse event (a "sentinel event") as being on "Accreditation Watch." This approach, adapted from the financial community's application of the "credit watch" concept, in essence reserved judgment on the organization and placed primary emphasis on the organization's in-depth review (known as a "root cause analysis") of the occurrence. The eventual definition of an acceptable root cause analysis and the effective engagement of affected organizations in this process were major pluses in advancing the medical error reduction initiative. However, the Accreditation Watch designation rapidly became problematic because, despite its intended neutrality, it, too, was viewed as negative labeling of organizations by the Joint Commission.

This led to the third iteration of the Sentinel Event Policy, which was adopted in late 1997 and implemented the following spring. This version contemplated the voluntary reporting of sentinel events and the subsequent root cause analyses, and promised confidentiality protections for this information. To our surprise, the new policy, which had carefully been subjected to prior field review, led to an eruption of protests across the hospital field.

What was the problem?

We had, unwittingly, for the first time placed on the healthcare organization's CEO the onus of making the decision as to whether or not to report a sentinel event to the Joint Commission. What this did was raise the legitimate concern that sharing such information, particularly the root cause analysis, with the Joint Commission might result in the waiver of confidentiality protections under existing state peer review protection statutes and expose these organizations to increased liability.

What to do?

After extensive consultation with legal experts in the field, the Joint Commission fashioned a series of reporting alternatives, which can be summarized as follows:

- send the information to us in the mail;
- bring the information to the Joint Commission, review it with us, and take it back home;
- have the Joint Commission visit the organization and review the root cause analysis;
- have the Joint Commission visit the organization and ask questions about the sentinel event and the root cause analysis; or
- have the Joint Commission visit the organization, inquire about changes in policies and procedures following the sentinel event, and review its process for conducting a root cause analysis.

So far, the latest system is working, at least on a modest level. We have almost 800 sentinel events and related root cause analyses in our database; 333 of these were reported last year. We issue quarterly advisories on sentinel events—Sentinel Event Alerts—that describe organizational lessons learned for specific types of sentinel events and suggest specific steps that can be taken to prevent such occurrences in other organizations. There is already good evidence that this information (particularly the suggestion that concentrated potassium chloride be removed from inpatient units) has reduced the incidence of certain types of sentinel events.

By the time the Institute of Medicine (IOM) released its report on medical errors late last year, the Joint Commission was already a veteran player in this arena.

Earlier this year, our board of commissioners framed what is now viewed as the definitive public policy position on the reporting of medical errors. It states that reporting systems, whether mandatory or voluntary, should have the following characteristics:

- events to be reported must be well defined and, if to a mandatory system, limited to serious adverse events;
- reports of serious adverse events must include the findings of the root cause analyses of these events;
- all information reported must be legally protected from disclosure;

- all accountable healthcare quality oversight bodies having a legitimate "need to know" must have full and timely access to the data and information in any reporting system; and
- information must be disseminated to the field that facilitates learning about medical errors and implementation of actions to improve patient safety.

The last chapters on the Joint Commission's Sentinel Event Policy and on the multiple other initiatives to reduce medical errors are still a long way from being written. But progress is being made. We have learned a lot about error and adverse event prevention, and more is being learned every day. And the IOM report has sensitized both the public and the provider community about the need to make resolution of this problem a top priority. So we are hopeful about the future.

The primary lessons we have learned in dealing with this issue clearly have broad applications for all healthcare enterprises.

- Policy must be grounded in the organization's mission and values.
- If there is just cause for a policy—if it is the right thing to do—the organization must be persistent and tenacious in assuring its full and effective implementation.
- Leadership matters in designing and implementing ground policy; the organization's staff and board look to the CEO to provide visionary policy direction.

Dr. O'Leary is a physician and president of the Joint Commission on Accreditation of Healthcare Organizations in Oakbrook Terrace, Illinois.

Strategy

Scott S. Parker

AT ONE POINT in my career, I relocated to become administrator of a small community hospital in Mesa, Arizona. The hospital was undersized and unable to meet the needs of a growing community. It needed to be totally replaced.

Shortly before I had been hired, the not-for-profit hospital's board of trustees had been deeply concerned about the future of the hospital. As a result, they released the administrator, the director of nursing, and the chief financial officer from their positions on the same day. They wanted a new leader who would be given the responsibility to organize the financing and then oversee the construction of a new replacement hospital.

The situation was as follows. The old hospital had accumulated a cash reserve of approximately $1 million, but the estimated cost of the new hospital was over $20 million. Realizing that they were woefully underfunded, the board of trustees had placed into motion the creation of a hospital taxing district, designed to facilitate the financial guarantee required to use tax exempt bond financing. The creation of a special hospital taxing district, however, necessitated referendum approval from the local voters living within the boundaries of the proposed district. I was recruited the same year the referendum for the hospital taxing district was held. As soon as I walked through the doors, I was immediately faced with the responsibility of organizing a political campaign in support of the referendum while, at the same time, recruiting a new management team.

I started the political process by personally meeting with nearly every community group and with influential individuals living in Mesa and Tempe, whose city boundary lines made up the boundaries of the proposed hospital taxing district. In that process, I discovered that there was a retired rancher living in Mesa who had spent his entire life opposing special taxing districts in his home state of Kansas. This political activity had become his avocation and he had established a successful track record in organizing community opposition to various taxing district proposals. Because of his retired status, he had ample time, energy, and determination to take on a new political cause, which had now become the proposed new hospital taxing district. As a "committee of one," he took it upon himself to knock on the door of each home in the city of Mesa, claiming significant increases in property taxes would be necessary to make up the deficits. The "man from Kansas" was making his argument well known and had caught the attention of the local media.

I met with the popular tax protester and attempted to persuade him that there would be no need for property tax increases because the hospital would be self-sufficient financially. While he was respectful and appreciative of the visit, he could not be moved from his opposition. The hospital district was going to continue to be the focus of his political initiative. Looking back, I realize that I should have engaged a political consultant to assist in the process.

When the day of the referendum vote came, I was still optimistic about the result, but the bond issue was defeated. I was devastated by the result, as were the members of the board of trustees, the employees, and the members of the medical staff. I remember the slow drive to the hospital from my home the morning after the election, wondering what I was going to say to the trustees and to the other members of our "hospital family." Clearly I would be asked, "What are we going to do now?" The problem was, I didn't know. I had been guilty of not developing a contingency plan. I could only state that, within 60 days, we would announce a new approach to financing the hospital.

About mid-morning, I decided I needed some time to myself to think through some alternatives. As I sat in my office, having requested a hold on all calls and visits, I asked myself if any of my previous experiences or observations might serve as a guide to try to develop some reasonable alternatives to our current crisis. I thought of my mentor, Stan Nelson, who once stated that few great new ideas are ever realized while sitting behind one's own desk. His counsel was to "get up and get out," and to stay fresh and receptive to new ideas. Then I remembered how Stan had initiated a successful merger between his hospital, Northwestern Hospital in Minneapolis, and Abbott Hospital, a neighboring competing facility. The merger had brought together the strengths of a larger hospital and the superb medical staff from a smaller hospital. Why couldn't I do something similar?

We needed the capital strength of a larger and stronger hospital, which could only be obtained if our smaller hospital were merged into a larger organization. It became clear to me that a merger with a large hospital in Phoenix and then the subsequent construction of a satellite hospital in Mesa and Tempe would be a potential answer to the current crisis.

I had only been in Arizona for a few months and I was not all that familiar with Phoenix hospitals or their CEOs. It was well understood, however, that the strongest hospital in the state was the Good Samaritan Medical Center located in downtown Phoenix, run by Steve Morris, a well-known and highly regarded CEO. I had met him socially on one or two occasions, so I simply called and asked him if he would be willing to meet with me to discuss some ideas about our two hospitals. With his busy calendar, it was several weeks before the meeting could be scheduled, but the delay gave me an opportunity to describe the concept I had in mind to our own board of trustees to gain their support for the idea.

When I met with Steve Morris and described our situation and made our proposal, he was enthusiastic in his initial response, thus enabling us to move forward. Surprisingly, we reached an agreement in concept regarding the basic principles of the merger quite easily. Both organizations were enthusiastic in their support, and both boards were willing to accept the merger and implement it within a few months in order to respond to the need for expediency in moving forward with a new hospital.

The merger resulted in the building of a new state-of-the-art hospital on the border of Mesa and Tempe, which became known as the Desert Samaritan Hospital. Good Samaritan and Desert Samaritan formed the nucleus of what eventually became the nationally known Samaritan Health System.

Looking back, I realize I learned the importance of having a backup contingency plan in place in case the priority strategy cannot be implemented. I also learned certain situations will arise that require expert counsel from experienced consultants, as was the case during the Mesa/Tempe political initiative. Since then I've called upon consultants and professional political strategists on several occasions.

I also learned that out of adversity arises great opportunity. Even with the disappointment of the lost election and the sense of desperation that resulted out of the crisis, there evolved a viable approach to financing. Today we not only have a new hospital, but also an integrated multihospital delivery system, which came to be considered one of the premier systems of its kind during the 1980s.

Great ideas can come out of adversity and its rippling effect. Every difficult situation has within it an opportunity for creativity if there is a willingness to take risk and innovate—traits that define the successful leader.

Mr. Parker was the president and CEO for Intermountain Health Care in Salt Lake City, Utah, from 1975 to 1999 and chairman of the American Hospital Association board of trustees in 1986.

Strategy

Boone Powell, Jr., FACHE

DURING MY CAREER I recall some important strategic challenges that were managed with carefully made decisions followed up by action. One strategic issue involved our corporate objective to build and strengthen alliances with our physicians.

As part of our strategic objective, we created our primary care group, the Health Texas Physicians Network, as a 501(a)-type organization. This type of network, with its corporate practice of medicine, allowed us to get around the barrier of expanding our network of physicians and then relying on the physicians to capitalize their needs. Because it is not reasonable to ask them to do that, the 501(a)-type organization gave us the advantage of being able put up the capital to create the network.

Health Texas Physicians Network has been operating now for six years. Our initial group of about a dozen family practitioners led to, principally, an internal medicine group. It was based in another hospital system, but they wanted to join us with their 30 physicians. That led to the formation of a large group on the main campus, Baylor. We then moved to the west (Irving). Before you knew it, about a year and a half later, we had the makings of a very fine network of top-line internists and primary care physicians.

We made the investment and bought those early practices but after that it was not necessary to purchase. The groups joined us. We might purchase assets, charts, or something, but after that point we merged others into our network. When it was all said and done, we ended up, several years later, with 45 different sites

The other thing we found was that recruiting the new graduates to our infrastructure was easy. The leaders of our group would go out and simply guarantee the first year salary; after that they were on their own. We stayed out of the productivity issues and operating losses because of the way it was structured. In 1999, we brought in about 40 physicians and another 30 in 2000.

There are a couple of things we've done with specialists that involved strategy. One was in 1993–94, where we worked out an arrangement with a large oncology group. They allowed us to merge our outpatient business with them, and then the group leased our outpatient cancer space from us. Baylor became a significant owner of the merged organization. In fact, the group went public in 1994 and subsequently merged last year with American Oncology Resources to create US Oncology. They care for between 13 and 15 percent of all cancer patients in the United States. We are the only provider organization that has any kind of relationship with them.

In January of 2000, another strategic effort was realized with the groundbreaking ceremony for our new heart hospital. We are building a separate licensed hospital in partnership with over 40 cardiologists. It took us over two years to find the right model and round up the physicians.

All three major cardiology groups and the peripheral vascular surgery physicians will come with us. That is very important where we live because the competitive model is the MedCath model and similar groups. We have taken the two biggest areas of healthcare required in hospitals (oncology and cardiology) and have the physicians tied to us. The next strategy we are working on is how to do something with orthopedics.

Looking back, I'm proud to say we stated up front what we wanted to do. As the chairman of Health Texas said, he couldn't think of one time where Baylor made a commitment on which they hadn't followed through. Therefore, if I had to give a piece of advice to other leaders,

I'd say you have to build everything on relationships and trust. This is a relationship business, not a transaction business.

I think from our strategies I can say that the smartest way to try and run healthcare organizations today is to find collaborative ways of doing so with your physicians.

Mr. Powell was the president and CEO *of Baylor Health Care System in Dallas, Texas from 1980 to 2000 and chairman of the Texas Hospital Association in 1998.*

Strategy

Elena Rios, M.D.

THIS IS A story of vision, opportunity, and perseverance, culminating in the birth of the National Hispanic Medical Association in 1994. It was a journey that began in California in the late 1960s when a group of activist Hispanic college students obtained a grant from the federal government to create the National Chicano Health Organization. These students were interested in expanding healthcare career opportunities for individuals from the Latino community so they could ultimately serve its neglected population. They had no idea at the time that their modest goals would spawn a broader vision for Hispanic participation in the mainstream of American medicine.

The promising organization disbanded in the 1970s, however, when the grant expired. However, the seed had been planted, and the leaders perpetuated the vision as they completed their education and moved into various communities around the country.

My involvement began in the early 1970s when I was an undergraduate premedical student at Stanford University and as a graduate student in public health at UCLA.

Many of the original leaders enlisted others in the cause over the years and helped create local and regional organizations that began the second-generation attempt to affect the Hispanic health agenda.

In the 1980s, Latino medical students took up the cause as they formed organizations designed to foster communication and serve as information exchange networks. I was a founder of the California

72

Chicano/Latino Medical Student Association in 1982. In 1989, I was an adviser at the start of the National Network of Latin American Medical Students, which helped to bring five regional groups back under one national umbrella.

The third generation in the development process commenced with the creation of the Chicano/Latino Medical Association of California in the early 1990s. I served as its second president beginning in 1991. This association expanded the scope of its forerunner organizations by developing a database of demographic information for members; educational topics and opportunities for Hispanic physicians, medical students, and other healthcare workers; and acted as a clearinghouse for career positions. The cause was furthered through the support of then–U.S. Surgeon General, Antonia Novello, M.D., at her national conference in 1991.

The next step toward the creation of a national Hispanic alliance in medicine began through my involvement in health policy research and activities in the Clinton/Gore campaign in 1991 and 1992. I was asked to put together a meeting of Hispanic health experts for the transition team. I identified key leaders from my past connections within the various Hispanic regional organizations and used their feedback on specific issues as I participated in the Healthcare Reform Task Force in 1993. After the task force completed its work, I went to work for the Office of Women's Health in Washington where, during the next four years, I was able to continue to develop a network of health policy–minded Hispanic leaders.

After 25 years of effort, we actually incorporated the first nationwide organization of Hispanic physicians in 1994: the National Hispanic Medical Association (NHMA). This organizing effort included establishing a board of directors and a national advisory committee of physicians from key cities where regional meetings were held.

The first annual conference of the NHMA was a modest one, held in 1997. In the three years since that meeting, our conference has grown to over 500 participants and has had speakers from the White House; the U.S. Surgeon General, Dr. David Satcher; the NIH director, Dr. Ruth Kirschstein; Office of Minority Health director, Dr. Nathan Stinson; and the Commonwealth Fund president. Several Hispanic physician speakers focused on cultural competence, clinical updates to eliminate health disparities for Hispanics, health policy, and career opportunities.

The scope of the organization continues to grow. While we are still a small organization with limited resources and a modest-sized staff, we continue our journey toward becoming a comprehensive voice and resource for physicians and other caregivers of Hispanic origin. Our ultimate goals are to:

- improve Hispanic health in the United States;
- support the career advancement of Hispanic physicians;
- be a resource for U.S. government healthcare policymakers;
- provide continuing education, training, and networking opportunities for Hispanic physicians; and
- become a full-fledged participant in organized medicine through involvement as a member of the American Medical Association House of Delegates and other established organizations.

We are certainly a long way from being all we can be. We are proud, however, of how much has been accomplished because of the vision and perseverance of many dedicated Hispanic leaders.

The lessons of this journey are universal, and I believe are critical to the success of any developing organization. My advice is to:

- identify leaders with energy and vision;
- understand the cultural differences of your constituents;
- understand that each constituency has its own priorities and agendas;
- have patience and realize that the growth and development of new ideas and/or organizations come in incremental steps that take time; and
- remember that the success or failure of the organization will depend on how well you network with others, who may be supportive or not, and your ability to gain their acceptance in the healthcare arena.

Dr. Rios is president of the National Hispanic Medical Association in Washington, DC.

Strategy

Elliott C. Roberts, Sr., CHE

BESIDES SERVING AS CEO of Charity Hospital in New Orleans, I have worked for New York City's Health & Hospitals Corporation, Detroit General Hospital, Chicago's Cook County Hospital, and other healthcare organizations. When I look back at my career, one challenge in particular was especially daunting: how to achieve the goals of a hospital when it involved legislative action. This was a significant strategic problem that occurred during the time I served as the Assistant Secretary of the Louisiana Department of Health and Hospitals and as CEO of Charity Hospital.

Charity Hospital in New Orleans was one of nine acute care hospitals that comprised the Charity Hospital System of the State of Louisiana. It was the largest and was considered the flagship of the system.

The Charity Hospital System, owned and operated by the State of Louisiana, suffered all the typical ills of politics and legislative restrictions, which limited the effectiveness of its operation in a dynamic healthcare delivery environment.

One of the most challenging aspects of my career was juggling "political footballs" in a highly politicized environment. As the political officeholders changed, my job or at least my ability to effect change in my job was sometimes threatened, and other times secured. One period stands out in my mind.

By gubernatorial appointment, I was made CEO of Charity in Louisiana. However, when the governor who appointed me was voted out of office, I was out of a job. His new Secretary of the Department of Health and Human Services had his own ideas about who should be CEO. Luckily, I was recruited to Chicago, where I eventually became the director of Cook County Hospital.

A few years later the governor who had appointed me CEO of Charity won reelection and he asked me if I would return to Louisiana and my old position as CEO of Charity. I accepted.

However, there is more to the story.

Although I was glad to be back at Charity, the problem was again the job stability factor. I knew the elections still determined whether or not I could keep my post.

It was the late 1980s with another election approaching, and I didn't know who was going to win. As usual, I tried planning for the changing of the guard, but without a clear-cut winner predicted, I needed to do something to provide more job stability should another governor take office.

I decided to partner with some stakeholders in Charity's success and collectively demonstrate vision, leadership, and strategy for our hospital. Specifically, we wanted to describe the need to change the system for the benefit of the patients we served as well as to increase management's effectiveness in the day-to-day operation. I collaborated with the chancellors of the two medical schools that had major teaching affiliation agreements with Charity—Louisiana State University Medical School and Tulane University Medical School—and we wrote a proposal in the form of a white paper. Our intent was to present this document to the successful candidate of the upcoming gubernatorial race. In the process of creating our proposal, we were careful to involve several external stakeholders within the community served to assure a buy-in. This included members of the legislature who also represented the hospital by virtue of its service to their districts' constituents.

The election was held and a new governor took office. I learned my appointment as CEO of Charity would be continued, but the proposal by now was about much more than my job security. It was about changing the system for the good of the patients and the system. So we arranged a visit with the new governor and presented our proposal. He accepted our proposal with an air of caution and reservation.

Although the governor seemed lukewarm to the idea, by this time we had no intention of letting it die just because we didn't have the governor's full support. So we obtained backing from a legislator from the House of Representatives and a senator to introduce our proposal in the form of legislation to create a separate organization—a public benefit corporation for Charity Hospital of Louisiana at New Orleans.

The bill was introduced, sailed through a few committees, approved on the House floor, and sent to the Senate for final ratification when the governor stepped in. Apparently, he never expected the bill to get as far as it did and killed it. His explanation was that he didn't want to separate "Big Charity," as Charity in New Orleans was called, from the rest of the system. Instead, the governor charged his secretary of Health and Human Services to come up with an alternate plan that included all hospitals in the Charity System. His secretary proceeded to assemble people to develop an alternate plan, but fortunately the legislation had named me as a member of the planning committee. Thus, I did end up having a role in the design and creation of the system's new structure, which ended up being The Louisiana Health Care Authority.

This is not the end of the story.

Toward the end of the process of creating this new plan, the gubernatorial elections were held again and the governor's post changed hands once more. Although my position seemed secure, politics as usual took over the process of selecting candidates for the Health Care Authority's board. Instead of having all qualified applicants, the list of proposed board members were laced with the governor's political friends. The Board's composition suffered. The Authority subsequently functioned ineffectively and had a poor relationship with the legislature, whose support it needed to exist. These factors caused the eventual collapse of the Louisiana Health Care Authority.

That's the end of the story.

Looking back, I see things I would have done differently. I would have taken into account that the limited expression of support by the governor probably meant he was not ready to commit to such a drastic proposed change. I would have constantly communicated with the governor and all key decision makers during the process of developing our proposal. Had I done that, perhaps I would have seen the red flags that adverse actions would be taken to derail the process unless we made changes.

My lessons learned may be valuable to other healthcare executives who must not only problem solve to effectively manage and lead successful medical enterprises, but for their very survival. It takes determination, patience, and fortitude just to survive in this dynamic healthcare arena.

My advice is to bring a vision to the organization and establish achievable objectives around that vision. This requires building a management team and requisite resources to accomplish the objectives. Build in controls and checkpoints to monitor the process and minimize problems. Problems will occur, but they must be handled swiftly and effectively.

Overall, managers and leaders must be flexible to be able to shift gears when external forces warrant. The shifting of plans must be done with confidence and determination to keep your management team on track.

Mr. Roberts is a professor in the department of preventive medicine and public health at Louisiana State University Medical School and was on the American Hospital Association board of trustees from 1971 to 1976.

Strategy

John A. Russell, FACHE

I LEARNED MANY strategic lessons from the assault on hospitals' tax-exempt status in Pennsylvania. It began in the late 1980s when municipalities and school districts throughout Pennsylvania began to challenge the tax-exempt status of hospitals with regard to property taxes in their communities. Literally dozens of communities filed suit against their hospitals, asking that the hospitals be added to the tax roles of the community for property taxation.

Our approach to the problem, as a statewide trade association representing all the hospitals in Pennsylvania, was to put together a "SWAT team" of professionals and consultants. The team consisted of legal counsel, public relations consultants, financial analysts, and experienced leaders that would move into each community and aid the challenged hospital in developing strategies and action plans to combat the community's pro-taxation initiatives. The team assisted each hospital in developing its overall strategy and action plan.

Although all of our efforts were well developed and well received by the hospitals, they lost their battles and our efforts failed. The hospitals were defeated in the courts. After 18 months of the ill-fated SWAT strategy, we needed to develop a creative new approach. We needed to change the law and help the hospitals to regain community support.

A new approach was developed with the help of a 22-member "Blue Ribbon Panel" comprised of leading hospital chief executives and trustees from throughout Pennsylvania. We spent 1990 conducting a series of intensive meetings to craft the leadership plan. The new plan,

Vision 2000, was designed to position hospitals to assume leadership in creating a new health system in Pennsylvania. The new system's mission would be to improve the health of the individuals and the communities served by each hospital. Our new strategy adopted a four-phased approach:

Phase I: Adoption of the plan by most of the hospitals in the state (1991).

Phase II: Education and training sessions to help hospitals in implementing the plan in their communities (1992–93).

Phase III: Promotion of community-based models throughout the state (1994).

Phase IV: Creation of a new organization to lead the "The Institute for Healthy Communities" initiative (1995).

Phases I and II were carried out successfully. Our goal was to change the behavior of the hospitals and to reposition them as part of the fabric of their communities through "Healthy Community" initiatives. To do so, we needed to have these intensive training sessions to identify community health needs and to create successful programs to address them. One of the major efforts involved recruiting teams of citizens from communities to participate in educational sessions. We wanted people to learn about the plan, to embrace it, to help design a health improvement plan for their communities, and help launch specific initiatives when they returned to their communities.

Phase III saw the creation of regional, then statewide, models to serve as learning laboratories. The first Healthy Communities Summit was held, and representatives from more than 60 communities attended.

Phase IV involved the Healthy Communities movement, which required a statewide resource center and support organization. As a result, the hospital association restructured itself into the Health Alliance of Pennsylvania and created five subsidiaries that worked together to create The Institute for Healthy Communities. Today all are working in partnership to lead Vision 2010.

The Pennsylvania law needed to be changed, and after a nine-year battle, the Association was successful in getting effective changes passed.

Here are some of the lessons I learned that are worth sharing:

- Complex problems can take you in many directions, so you need to know your vision and values in trying to solve these problems, and use the experience to implement solutions you care about.
- A tax crisis can serve as a catalyst for transforming how healthcare is practiced and delivered in your state as it did in Pennsylvania.
- You can't win an economic argument in the courts if hospital behavior does not support the not-for-profit basis upon which tax exemption was created.
- The most important events in your career may be crises. How you deal with each crisis determines your management career.
- Healthcare reform presents many opportunities for today's leaders who must create around the needs of people, not institutions.
- Recognize that it is a great time to be a healthcare leader—go look for problems to solve!

Mr. Russell is the chairman of the Pennsylvania Institute for Healthy Communities and was on the American Hospital Association board of trustees from 1990 to 1993.

Strategy

C. Thomas Smith, Jr., CHE

VHA IS A NATIONAL alliance of community-owned healthcare organizations and affiliated physicians. Its members are committed to making a difference in the quality of lives for those they serve. For more than two decades, the organization has used multiple strategies to help its members adapt to changing environmental circumstances and to succeed in their markets. Early in my time as president/CEO at VHA, I encountered a strategic challenge that required the changing of some old paradigms.

After I came on board, part of my responsibility was to analyze the organization's old paradigms and help shape new ones to lead the organization toward success. Early in the life of the alliance, a decision was made to create local offices scattered across the country to assist shareholder and member organizations in structuring themselves around a local marketplace. It sounded good on paper, but after this structural plan was in place, it proved to be far from perfect. Among the problems was a wedge that seemed to exist between the staff members in the corporate office and those in the field. The degree of estrangement varied and reflected, somewhat, the personal styles and agendas of local leaders. Nevertheless, there was a general dysfunctionality between the 29 local offices and the parent organization.

In organizations where there are multiple sites of service, there are natural disconnections that arise—differences in priorities, personal agendas, variations in style. All of this created an enormous barrier to progress. Members typically identified with their local office, with which they had far more intimate contacts. Some local office staff chose, for various reasons, not to support national initiatives, but to shelter their members from these goals and programs when they deemed it appropriate. The result, of course, was an organization filled with frustration on both the national and local level, with each side believing the other neither understood the real issues nor had the interests of members foremost.

The gravity of the situation demanded resolution, as maintaining the status quo was the sure formula for failure, or at least mediocre performance.

Accordingly, a task force was assembled, including senior executives from both the national and local offices, which was led by an executive vice president who had founded the first local office and was VHA's most senior employee. A strategic planning/organizational development consultant was also retained to assist the group with clarity about the mission and strategies, while crafting the appropriate structure to achieve them.

Perspectives of the task force members on how to effect change ranged from the national organization sending more resources to local offices "so they could do what they believed was right," to the elimination of the local office model.

Considerable thought and energy went into understanding the issues at hand and seeking a solution that was both in the best interests of members and of the alliance. It was apparent that the offices had evolved in a rather natural way as separate miniature corporate entities with their own boards and local executives accountable to them. It also became apparent that that model spawned some bad habits on both sides. For example, a few local executives had trouble embracing the national sponsorship and used the organizational separation as a shield to behaviors that were in their interest, but not necessarily in the alliance's best interest. On the other hand, some national program managers simply bypassed local offices and approached members directly, creating opportunities for misunderstanding by both members and staff.

After months of deliberations, three alternative models to the prior franchise-like model were devised. Over a three-year period, national and local staff worked with local boards to evaluate options and select one that seemed best suited for each local circumstance.

After several years of work, I'm proud to share that the 29 VHA-licensed offices now number 18, reflecting multiple consolidations, with 11 of them functioning as wholly owned subsidiaries of the national organization, 3 as relicensed entities with clear mutual obligations, and 4 maintaining their old status.

Additional changes may occur in the next few years, and we are ready to adapt.

The result of recreating and modifying the structure of our entity has been a considerable change in the atmosphere and attitude between the field office leadership and the national organization. For example, all of the office leaders participate as peers in the national organization's leadership group that meets regularly as a senior management executive council. Local and national leaders jointly shape annual and multiyear goals and share in the same incentive compensation structure. There is much greater coherency of purpose and consistency in priorities than in the previous decade.

The result of these positive changes is that VHA continues to grow in both membership and in programmatic content, and most importantly, in the amount of service provided to our membership. We have greatly expanded the reach of the organization into our healthcare organizations and have redefined the alliance from being dominantly a group purchasing organization to an organization that provides group purchasing services along with support for clinical improvement, operational performance, and market share success. None of this could have happened if we had not realigned priorities, incentives, and performance of the national team with the local team.

The natural dissonance, which exists when organizations have multisite operations, must be overcome by constant vigilance and communication, clarity of purpose, and mutual respect. Any breach in those areas will create irreparable harm that can severely damage an organization's ability to achieve its mission. It is counterproductive, unrewarding, and uncomfortable to have teammates who are at odds. These "teammates," half of whom do not support the organization's purpose and strategies, and all of whom are not willing to help build a culture based on mutuality of interest and respect, drag down the organization. In these instances, change is inevitable.

Problems such as this one typically develop over a long period of time, and they are not easily eradicated. Indeed, the amount of time that goes into changing old habits is expensive, and the effort required is enormous.

I learned several lessons from this experience. I now know that the key to resolving problems is for us, as leaders and managers, to keep a constant focus on our mission, our commitment to bring value to our members, and on the set of values that define how we work together. Lack of attention to any of these, in my judgment, compromises our ability to make changes that will be sustainable over the long haul.

If teammates share a common vision and a set of values rooted in personal dignity and mutual respect, as well as being good stewards in always doing what's right for those served, then the odds of creating a workable solution are greatly enhanced.

Mr. Smith is the president and CEO *of* VHA, *Inc., in Dallas, Texas and was the chairman of the American Hospital Association board of trustees in 1991.*

Strategy

Robert J. Wright, FACMPE

MY FIRST JOB in healthcare management came as a result of a new office manager's failure to show up on her first day on the job. I was working with a credit bureau and happened to have been calling on the office that fateful day. In a passing conversation, one of the physicians asked me if I knew how to be a practice administrator, and I responded, "I don't know, but I think I can figure it out if you give me the job." Remarkably, they offered me that opportunity and the rest is history.

Our journey as a group started with three general practitioners. Since then, we have been involved in starting over 30 companies that have contributed to meeting the needs of the healthcare industry. Large conglomerates have since acquired several of these companies and they are now publicly traded enterprises.

One of our finest contributions to our patients and physicians was the construction of Medical City Dallas.

As with most opportunities, the essential tenet of Medical City Dallas was to address a need. Our physicians simply were unable to be efficient in their daily routines. It was apparent when you calculated just the daily time that was expended during the numerous trips back and forth between various hospitals and their offices, together with the travel time to and from their homes. Further, an inefficient office space design compounded their inefficient use of time. Essentially, we simply had an abundance of wasted time and therein was a chance for improvement.

Our initial planning started with an assessment of where the physicians lived and how they would begin their day. Since most of them lived north of town, we focused our efforts toward identifying a work setting that would be closer to where they lived. We focused on a plan that would make our physicians efficient in the use of their time. We were insistent on avoiding the conventional medical office layout. Also, the physicians wanted any new facility to be a taxable entity. They did not want to ask the community for donations for its development.

In addition to what our physicians needed, our patients also had expectations for convenience. In order to address the needs of both physicians and patients, we were confronted with a fair share of challenges in the design and formation of the ideal facility. Moreover, we wanted a scheme that our patients would find pleasant, appealing, and convenient. We wanted it to be unique, and we demanded functionality.

Next, our efforts to acquire financing from an insurance company were fraught with problems because these institutions did not typically loan money to hospitals. However, after we successfully leased the facility to a hospital management company, we found a company that was optimistic about financing the transaction. Although more commonplace today, this was a unique solution in those days.

Reflecting on these past 30 years, I am convinced that the best partnerships are those that are formed by the blending of the unique talents and skills of both parties. This is particularly powerful when each party is totally committed to the success of the other. In other words, everyone wins or no one wins. This win-win formula promotes energy, focus, respect, and mutual trust, which in turn yields the greatest results. Such is the partnership we have had with Trammell Crow over the years. Trammell was a very successful real estate developer, while our group brought an understanding of the efficiency needs for a medical facility. From my experience, qualities that form the foundation for success are the partnerships that are grounded in mutual respect, honesty, openness, and the sincere commitment to make everyone in the relationship successful.

Our focus has been, and continues to be, that of looking for the needs of those we serve and making all participants successful in the outcome. It's an endearing quality to work with people who aspire to bring value to those they serve.

Our perspective and passion to serve were the fundamental ingredients that resulted in a "medical city" with retail shopping, banking, database answering service, computerized communication equipment, concierge service, restaurants, dry cleaners, physician offices, and an acute care hospital, all under one roof. And what a comfortable roof it is—the atriums and balconies form the aesthetic foundation for a warm environment. Art shows, flower displays, and automobile exhibits are only a few of the special events that make the environment entertaining as well as functional. We have learned a lot from the successes of our initiatives and from the failures of some of our efforts as well.

It is so clear to me that excitement and a passion for your ideas and your work is essential. In fact, one individual once called me the "Oral Roberts" of healthcare, and an entrepreneur described me as the "Billy Graham" of medicine. That description came from a Christian Scientist who ultimately invested in one of our business initiatives. He was sold on our idea as a result of our "pure excitement" for the project and our convincing commitment to make it successful.

Finally, professionals need to control their own destiny. Never stop looking for ways to improve on the service you owe each customer. Never stop problem solving and never stop seeking new and innovative solutions for the needs of your customer. It is by addressing these needs and in the solving of problems that you will have the opportunity to create. It is what lies in this creation that becomes the fuel and energy for professional challenge and success.

Mr. Wright is the president of Medical Cities, Inc. in Dallas, Texas. He was president of the American College of Medical Practice Executives in 1980 and president of the Medical Group Management Association in 1976.

PART II

OPERATIONS

Introduction

"Thunder is good, thunder is impressive; but it is the lightning that does the work."   —Mark Twain

IT IS DOUBTFUL that Mark Twain was describing the need of healthcare organizations to maintain a daily focus on efficient and effective operations when he scribbled these words. Regardless, the image works. It is imperative that organizations maintain an enlightened focus on operations and the needs of those they serve: the patient. It is clear that operations are the lightening of healthcare organizations. From effective operations comes the trust and credibility for managers and leaders to develop strategic initiatives and plans that form the basis for a group's future. But without the lightning, there will be no thunder.

Progressive leaders see operations as a cycle of cause-and-effect actions and relationships. As a result, from each operational procedure, policy, or decision comes an effect on the environment. Each action or transaction is vitally intertwined and the sum of all such activities makes the organization successful, or not. Individuals in these progressive organizations are trained and empowered to understand the nuances of the cause-and-effect phenomenon. From this global understanding, and with sensitivity to how each individual and function fits into the larger picture, there is the ability to communicate opportunities for continued improvement. There are no boundaries or territory in these organizations.

Organizations are only as strong as the people who work in them. Those people that are organized and function as disciplined and focused teams with a common goal are the most successful. Similar to winning sports teams, those organizational teams that "play in the zone" are the superstars. From an operational perspective, to play in the zone is to focus on the results of the present moment and spontaneously respond to the effect in a manner that has the most positive impact on the next encounter. All of this is done from the perspective of those who are served by the organization. The superstar teams are composed of individuals who enjoy working together. They have love and esteem for each other. And they understand how their efforts fit within the scope of the organization. They have respect for other teams throughout the organization and they are committed to helping others whenever they can.

"Best performers" establish and understand the operations work cycle and its six domains.

CORE MISSION AND VALUES

The best performers have a clear, concise core mission that is universally accepted by everyone in the organization and can be translated to everyone's job. There is a deep belief that the mission is noble and right and there is a passion to accomplish it each day. In addition, there is a set of values that provides the foundation for guiding the organization and for decision making. There is no compromise around the mission and values, nor is there a tolerance for behavior that is inconsistent with them.

"Have fun, don't take yourself too seriously, delegate responsibility, constantly learn, and when you're wrong, admit it."
—Ian S. Easton

"The experience taught me many lessons about managing competing interests and keeping patients' needs in the forefront during organizational change." —Robert W. Fleming

Knowledge, attitude, and behavior are the essential characteristics of the people charged with making an organization successful. But the more important of these is behavior! Best performers seek out people with consistent and positive behaviors. They appreciate and reward the performance of team members and seek out these people in their hiring practices.

"The team focused on implementing the game plan and on building a cohesive management team that had a system-first attitude."
—John G. King

"This situation . . . confirmed the value of preparation and teamwork in leading a successful healthcare organization."
—David R. Page

"The success we experienced confirmed my strong belief the organizations thrive though the efforts of what I term as high performance teams."
—Michael A. Wilson

LISTENING

As a part of their very culture, the best performers listen, learn, and change in order to improve on the goods and services they provide to those they serve. Moreover, they are convinced that they do serve at the will of their customers, clients, and patients. They understand that those served have options and they have a genuine commitment to retain and enhance their market share. The options for listening differ, but the translation of the knowledge gained to improve operational procedures, policies, and processes is a never-ending journey toward excellence.

"Communication between managers and associates must be solid so that the expertise and insights of all parties can be combined in the most effective way to reach the goals of the organization."
—Joseph P. Newhouse

"Listening was very important so that everyone felt they had an opportunity to place their position on the table."

—Gordon M. Sprenger

The best performers establish and measure performance targets. Targets are aggressive, but attainable. They celebrate the accomplishments of each success and they learn from the errors that are made. The culture of best performers is well defined. There is accountability throughout the environment, and there is mutual respect that everyone is doing his or her best to attain the mission. Rather than individuals, teams are recognized for the power of their work and their contributions to the success of the organization.

" . . . never forget that operations are where all of the strategies and activities of a medical group come together. A great idea poorly implemented is doomed to fail."   —Sara M. Larch

"My story . . . is a case study about the need to anticipate the outcome of certain actions and inaction."

—C. Thompson Hardy III

The best performers develop functional and effective strategic and work plans that focus on the essential elements that move the organization forward. These are no-frill plans that serve as a road map to the future. But as important, the best performers translate the plans into execution strategies that materialize as operational improvements. But, in addition, the best performers are willing and capable of taking advantage of opportunities that may randomly arise. Frequent and effective communications serve as the basis for a healthy environment.

"Much has been written about the failure of mergers . . . this is due, in general, to a failure in executing rather than an invalid strategy."

—Don L. Arnwine

"The practice was performing well, both operationally and financially, and physicians and staff seemed relatively content. Had we not been vigilant, however, that could have changed very quickly."
—Karen Buck

"The final analysis, however, is that it was just not run well form an infrastructure and operations standpoint."
—Mark R. Neaman

"While strategic planning is certainly important, it is often that serendipitious events have just as much of a long term impact on the organization as the most carefully thought out plan."
—Alan M. Stoll

QUALITY IMPROVEMENT

Quality improvement is a way of life for best performers. Operational improvement is a daily event and teams are encouraged, indeed expected, to alter processes and procedures in order to enhance outcomes and results. Best performers do not seek to blame, they seek to understand and change in order to improve. Excellence is an elusive goal, but it is an end that is constantly sought.

" . . . the long-term prosperity of any enterprise is not built on its intermediate successes, but rather on the organization's response to adversity."   —Joseph C. Hutts

" . . . we recognized very early that any measurable degree of success couldn't be achieved without improving the process of care delivery.   —Richard M. Scrushy

"The assessment of the data indicated that improvement in our communication with patients would improve satisfaction as well as the quality of care."   —Sandra W. Reifsteck

Operations

Don L. Arnwine

MUCH HAS BEEN written about the failure of mergers to produce their intended advantages in savings. It is my contention that this is due, in general, to a failure in execution rather than an invalid strategy.

One of the most difficult operational issues that arises following a merger of healthcare organizations is a consolidation of clinical services. A successful consolidation, however, is critical to achieving the intended advantages of a merger. In many instances, when there is a failure, it is the result of staffwide resistance.

I'd like to share an operational challenge I faced during my career when I was involved in consolidating clinical services following a merger. During the midpoint of my career, I became the first president and CEO of a new organization that resulted from the merger of five hospitals. The mergers occurred over a two- to three-year period and involved just over 1,000 beds.

The lessons come from the process we underwent in consolidating the services of the five hospitals.

All administrative services were consolidated and the consolidation of clinical services, where appropriate, was planned to follow. This plan for clinical consolidation was approved by the board with input from key physician leaders.

Soon, however, we encountered resistance from the physician specialties and nursing. The reasons for the resistance were general based on the following:

- disagreement with the concept of consolidation;
- personal inconvenience;
- fear of disruption;
- comfort with the present situation; and
- fear of change and the unknown.

In evaluating the wisdom of consolidating the various services we offered, we dealt with each department and the members of those departments. Thankfully, we had consolidated the medical staff organizations in advance. Having one Medical Executive Committee to work through was much more efficient and helpful than working with a separate committee from each of the hospitals.

As a part of the process, we used established criteria to determine the services that would be consolidated. We asked ourselves questions such as:

- Would the cost savings be significant enough to justify the change?
- Would it conserve the overall consumption of space?
- Would it result in an enhanced service from the standpoint of quality and/or capability?
- Would there be synergy between services located in the same facility?

Next we created working teams by discipline and established timelines for the consolidation project. Following the closure of two of the hospitals and the removal of acute care from a third, the problem was which services would be located in which of the two remaining major facilities. Because this consideration elicited a lot of conflict, we finally employed conflict resolution techniques.

Transportation between facilities became an issue for much of the staff. In response, commitments were made to add resources for that purpose.

It was eventually concluded that a general medical and general surgical capability would be important to maintain in each facility, but that all of the specialty services were candidates for consolidation. Radiology was, of course, maintained in each facility. But the specialty components of radiology were consolidated. The clinical laboratory was consolidated and arrangements were secured for transport of specimens from the other facilities to the central location.

We learned several things from the process of consolidating clinical services after the merger. The reason that clinical service consolidation most often fails results from the resistance and the conflict that this resistance creates. In our merger, consolidation was not accomplished with an "iron fist," but with involvement and buy-in. I think we were successful because there was a resolve from the board level, top management, and key physician leadership to see it through. When this became evident, a lot of the resistance and conflict throughout the ranks was overcome. As mentioned, it was also helpful to have just one Medical Executive Committee with which to build a medical consensus.

A principle lesson was that the promise of enhancement of the capability and quality of the service was much more important to gaining the consensus than the promise of cost savings. Staff are not motivated by how much money an organization will save. Given the early resistance in our newly formed organization and what worked in helping us overcome those barriers, I am convinced that physicians and nurses really do care about the capability and quality of services rendered to their patients. In fact, they will place it above their own self-interests when convinced that it will occur.

We accomplished our mission effectively in a fairly short period of time and in the process learned the value of follow through and "living up" to the promises that were made. This pattern has endured and worked well now for some 25 years in this particular situation.

I believe that the concept of unity and sharing between governance, management, physician partners, employees, and community are more important than they were in the past. The antidote to shrinking resources is expanded relationships.

Mr. Arnwine is the president and CEO of Arnwine Associates, a division of McManis Consulting, in Irving, Texas.

Operations

Karen Buck, FACMPE

WHILE IT IS important for healthcare executives to plan for the future and develop lasting relationships with physicians, staff, and community leaders, it is also critical to the survival of the organization that he or she continues to pay close attention to daily operations. This fact was driven home to me almost 15 years ago when I was the administrator of a small group practice.

While I monitored daily operations, many of the tasks of the clinic were shared with our assistant administrator, "Barbara," and our in-house accountant, "Suzanne." They had both been employed for enough time to be trusted members of the management team.

The practice was performing well, both operationally and financially, and physicians and staff seemed relatively content. Had we not been vigilant, however, that could have changed very quickly.

Barbara came to me one day after returning from a Medical Group Management Association meeting and expressed concern about an event that she remembered while the program speaker talked about the need to have good financial checks and balances. It seems that when I had been out of the office one day, Suzanne asked Barbara to sign a check for her without proper supporting documents. While it raised a bit of a red flag when it occurred, Barbara had not pursued it. We began to look into this particular incident and it led us to other irregularities. It quickly became clear that Suzanne had been embezzling money from the clinic for four or five months. The total amount was not large, but the $6,000 could have grown much larger if we had not discovered it then.

The method of embezzlement was somewhat unique because she did not collect cash and was not an authorized signatory on the bank account. However, she did visit our bank regularly and was well known and liked by the bank staff. Apparently, some months prior to our exposing the crime, Suzanne had gone to the bank and told them that the clinic had gotten into trouble with vendors for payment irregularities, and that some of them were now requiring us to pay our bills with money orders. Against bank policy, they gave her money orders with blank payee sections. She made them payable to fictitious payees and cashed them herself.

Our first step was to discreetly audit our financial records to confirm the embezzlement. We also talked with the bank about their mishandling of the money orders. Once the facts were established, I informed the president of the group and called the clinic's labor attorney. We constructed a carefully worded letter of termination to Suzanne, and I proceeded to advise her of our findings and deliver the termination letter at approximately noon.

Suzanne did not deny the allegations, and in fact expressed that she knew it was "only a matter of time" before she got caught. I directly supervised the collection of her personal belongings and escorted her out of the building.

About 4:30 p.m. that afternoon, I received a telephone call from her husband inquiring if something had happened at work that day. He was calling from the emergency room of the local hospital where Suzanne had been admitted for an overdose of medications and alcohol. When I explained the circumstances of the termination to him, he was very apologetic and immediately agreed to make restitution of the money that she had taken. Fortunately, she did recover and later received psychiatric treatment.

When we discovered the misdeed, there was no doubt that Suzanne had to be terminated, but we also had to decide whether or not to press for criminal prosecution. Because she was cooperative with us and agreed to repay the money, we chose not to pursue legal action.

This incident taught me never to take the safety of daily operations for granted. No matter how trusted employees may be, the system itself must have proper safeguards to prevent any temptation to misappropriate funds. Checks should be monitored by number, check stock should be kept secure, and there must be a separation of cash handling, check writing, and accounting functions. I would also suggest that the end of year audit by the outside accountant be thorough.

I also learned something about human resources management. Virtually all employment applications ask for a relative to notify in case of an emergency. We too often take this lightly. Because of the potential for self-harm, I now routinely call the relative named on the application whenever a severe discipline or termination takes place. This not only alerts the family of a potential problem, but will also likely protect the organization from legal action later.

My advice to medical administrators is twofold. First, top management must always be involved in daily operations enough to properly monitor the safety and security of business activities—not to the point of micromanaging, but enough to be vigilant. Second, top management must always be compassionate in administering the most difficult task of leadership—the termination of an employee. This will not only help you feel better, but may prevent an irreversible tragedy.

Ms. Buck is the executive director of the Casa Blanca Medical Group in Gilbert, Arizona and board chair of the American College of Medical Practice Executives for 2001.

Operations

Ian S. Easton, Ph.D., FACMPE

AT SOME POINT in their careers, most medical administrators are faced with the challenge of renovating an existing facility or constructing a new one. While the building project itself is ambitious enough, it is often the move that takes place later that creates most of the chaos. Therefore, planning for the move is very important.

In the late 1980s, I became the director of ambulatory services for an academic medical center. The center had already committed to construct a new facility of 500,000 square feet, of which 80 percent would be dedicated to ambulatory services. The other 20 percent was for support services, a cafeteria, and a new clinical laboratory.

As you can imagine, the size and complexity of the move was enormous. We planned to move 21 separate medical and surgical clinics, a clinical laboratory, outpatient pharmacy, a materials distribution center, the laundry, housekeeping, and a central mailroom. The number of employees affected by the move was over 1,200.

Recognizing the time and effort necessary to accomplish this monumental task, we began planning for the move at the commencement of construction rather than waiting until the building was nearly complete. This later proved to be a critical decision.

We created specific task forces to plan and facilitate the move, and dealt with such issues as:

- the purchase of new equipment and furniture involving over 15,000 items, ranging from a linear accelerator to individual trash cans;

- arranging for the timing of delivery of existing and new equipment to coincide with occupancy of the facility;
- deactivation of the existing facility after the move—turning in keys, relocating equipment and supplies, and so forth;
- staff orientation to the new facility, which included mock practice sessions;
- a training manual for staff, which included general and support services policies, patient flow, materials flow, and a map of the new building;
- physician orientation;
- a public relations program, including tours of the facility, several receptions, and mementos for attendees; and
- a move-day communications plan, which included procedures for reporting goods damaged in transit, coordinating the transfer of medications and narcotics, patient care management, and the move-day hot line.

We were able to accomplish the move with a minimum of disruption to clinical operations because of the diligence of our staff and our attention to detail well in advance of the move date.

Some of the key reasons we were successful:

- We appointed an overall move coordinator who had the authority to make decisions as required along the way.
- We appointed individual department coordinators who supervised the move and kept the move coordinator informed.
- We planned the move down to the minutest detail, for example, matching telephone jacks with telephones with the same number.
- We placed a six-month moratorium on changes or alterations to the new space unless there was a legitimate emergency. This negated the pressure to make wanted, but not needed, changes.
- We anticipated problems and addressed them as they arose.

The move went well. We were prepared for almost anything, but there were still some glitches. For example, some of the soap dispensers fell off the wall onto the faucets and into some sinks at night, turning on the water and covering up drains, eventually filling the basins and flooding rooms. We thought it was sabotage as it happened in four rooms in one week in the first month of occupancy. It turned out to be substandard workmanship, simply the result of poor installation.

The true message of my experience with moving is no different than many other situations that I have dealt with during a 30-year career in medical practice management:

- Have fun
- Don't take yourself too seriously
- Delegate responsibility
- Constantly learn
- When you're wrong, admit it

Dr. Easton is the head of the department of applied technology at Coastal Georgia College in Brunswick, Georgia and was the president of the American College of Medical Practice Executives in 1996.

Operations

Robert W. Fleming

ONE OF THE most significant strategic and operational challenges I have faced in my career was the integration of Saint Mary's Hospital and Rochester Methodist Hospital into the Mayo System. The experience taught me many lessons about managing competing interests and keeping patients' needs in the forefront during organizational change.

Both hospitals worked closely with the Mayo Clinic for many years, but did not become fully integrated into the System until 1985 and 1986. Saint Mary's opened in 1889 and grew over the years to become a 1,200-bed acute-care facility. Rochester Methodist Hospital was established in 1954, and by 1985 was an 800-bed institution. Both hospitals were closed staff, limited to the medical staff of Mayo Clinic, and only Mayo patients were admitted to these hospitals. The Mayo Clinic staff totaled 1,000 physicians and scientists. The integration was completed in June 1986.

The rationale for integration was twofold:

- to solidify the Mayo System's position in the national marketplace, and
- to become more responsive and efficient in the delivery of patient services.

Looking at the healthcare environment at the time, there were many changes underway. Historically, reimbursement to hospitals had been on a cost-plus basis, and to physicians on a fee-for-service basis. Diagnosis-related groups (DRGS), implemented in the fall of 1983, completely changed the incentives for hospitals. Hospitals and physicians became one of the few segments of the economy under price controls.

In this environment, Mayo concluded that decisions needed to be based on what was best for the patient and the medical center rather than what was best for Saint Mary's, Rochester Methodist, or Mayo Clinic. Because the DRG payment included Mayo Clinic services (e.g., laboratory, x-ray, physical medicine, respiratory therapy, ICU monitoring), it was necessary to negotiate with the hospitals about how to divide payments. As separate organizations with some competition between the hospitals, the potential for disagreement increased. In addition, the separate organizations disagreed about strategic and operational planning. Everything at issue could be resolved better if we were one organization instead of three.

Historically, individual patients decided where to obtain healthcare. However, as employers and the government became increasingly cost conscious, they played a bigger role in the decision. It was apparent that Mayo needed a unified competitive response to major purchasers who were interested in the charge for a package of services rather than paying for each line item. These changes in the healthcare environment led to the conclusion that it was time to agree to a formal merger to replace the informal arrangement between the hospitals and the clinic.

Many task forces developed plans to help the organizations work together more closely. The initial focus was on telecommunications, finance, human resources, information systems, communications, community relations, and development. Changes due to integration were gradual. All changes in the short term were at the upper management levels. Daily medical practice was continued as in the past. Saint Mary's Hospital retained its Catholic identity, and a sponsorship board was formed to support that identity.

As with most integrations and mergers, we underestimated the significant human issues involved in cultural integration. We underestimated the lingering effect of interfacility competitiveness and organizational allegiances. Some departments did not understand the significant differences between Clinic and hospital operational practices. Many assumed that if they could operate one entity, they could operate the other. We learned that bringing together separate policies and practices was critical to creating unity. One of the most important of these was a common salary and benefits system.

We learned other lessons from the integration process:

- Change at a pace that fits the extremes of cultural differences and competitiveness.
- Retaining departmental leadership from, and especially in, the separate institutions will further perpetuate the "old cultures."
- Gains can be achieved in patient care if:
  - standardized care is developed at both hospitals; and
  - the integration brings together common systems and aligns technology and people, eliminating barriers to moving the patient to the most appropriate care site.
- Collaboration can improve the working relationships of physicians, administrators, and nursing by:
  - fostering collegiality;
  - developing consensus; and
  - establishing expected behaviors.
- A single concept of resource allocation that does not separate technical and physician components is most efficient and viable.
- The senior level of leadership should be integrated to mirror the rest of the organization. Avoid exceptions.
- Use organizational development resources to assist with the cultural sensitivities.
- Proactively evaluate the success of integration rather than defaulting to evaluation as a reactive strategy.
- Consolidate the department leadership promptly (designating one person as the department head) to achieve single organization perspective. This approach can:

- achieve a critical mass of cultural agreement and provide avenues for subspecialization;
- provide a new team to define functions and structure; and
- keep everyone engaged.

"The needs of the patient come first" can serve as a guideline for building the structure and process of integration. This prevents development of a purely financial model of care delivery.

Mr. Fleming was associated with the Mayo Clinic in Rochester, Minnesota, for more than 30 years before retiring as the CEO in 1996. He was president of the Medical Group Management Association in 1984.

Operations

C. Thompson Hardy III, FACMPE

MY STORY IS one of failure resulting from too much success. It's also a case study about the need to anticipate the outcome of certain actions or inactions.

In 1981, I became the administrator of a 21-physician multispecialty group in Akron, Ohio. The group was in poor shape financially, but the job was appealing because of the potential for improving virtually all of the basic operating functions. I was ready to lead my own group, having worked for four years as the assistant administrator of a highly productive 70-plus physician clinic, and this seemed like the best opportunity for me to come in as a hero in my first senior management position.

Over the first five years of my tenure, we worked tirelessly to overhaul every operating system and department. Clinic supervisors eagerly assumed responsibility for turning around the performance in their work areas and enthusiastically supported and implemented the ideas that we jointly developed. Physician productivity and collections increased, accounts receivable decreased, overhead was cut, and physician incomes grew substantially. My role evolved into that of an innovator/facilitator rather than direct problem solver, as I encouraged more direct communication between supervisors and the physicians. It was a good strategy, because we made great strides as an organization.

While I was consumed with making basic functional improvements—and basking in the success of the results—the seeds of failure, as well as my own discontent, were being sown. As we achieved each success, our physician leadership became more and more complacent and thus resistant to change. It was as though they had gambled and won, and didn't want to gamble again for fear that they would lose it all. I tried to suppress my concern and frustration over our mishandled opportunities, but I knew in my heart that it was only a matter of time before it would surface. Three examples of our group's paralysis are illustrated in the following scenarios.

As the only group practice in the community, we had clear opportunities to grow, both in size and scope of specialties. Several local physicians approached us about joining the group, but we often rejected them for trivial reasons, despite the endorsement of the young physicians in the group and of myself. One case involved the first female physician to join us. She was a well-qualified dermatologist just out of training, and wanted to return to her hometown. It took enormous time and energy for me to convince the board that she and her specialty would benefit the group.

In another example, we were approached by a major insurance carrier who offered us exclusive provider status for one of the first capitated products to be introduced in the area. Two of the younger physicians and I undertook a major study and negotiation process, which culminated in what would have been a very beneficial contract for the group. The proposal was rejected, however, primarily from fear of a new reimbursement methodology, and I was criticized for the time and energy that I put into the project.

Finally, I can remember when a new physician in the OB/GYN department requested an ultrasound unit, which had been a standard tool in his residency training. The physician and I received the endorsement of the group's radiologist and demonstrated a positive economic impact. The board was afraid of making a large investment for a new, unproven physician and test modality, and demanded a sizeable 'group tax' on the revenues before approving the purchase. The investment turned out to exceed our expectations, but this issue became a major factor in that physician's resentment of the group's leadership, and later departure.

As time wore on, my management style changed. I began to address new ideas for the group, whether generated internally or externally, from a negative perspective. I looked for reasons that the board would reject them rather than how the proposal would benefit the organization. At the time, I rationalized that I was managing my expectations and the board process, but I now realize that I had given up on the group's ability to make key strategic decisions to position itself for the future.

I finally began to see that my time with the group was growing short as the board rejected two major strategic opportunities during my final two years at the clinic. One involved the development of an ambulatory surgical center/surgery office building on the clinic's campus, and the other was a purchase offer from a physician practice management company.

I realized my hands would be tied in leading the group forward. The board and I mutually agreed that I would move on after helping the group find a replacement.

Four years after my departure, the group, in essence, dissolved. At that time, the facilities and assets of the practice were turned over to the hospital, and the eleven physicians who remained with the group were relocated into the hospital's professional office building.

Although I believe that one or both of the final two initiatives they rejected would have prevented the group's demise, there were several factors that contributed to their failure.

- Because the clinic building and equipment were owned by a foundation, there wasn't any opportunity for physicians to build equity by expansion.
- One-third of the medical staff was in their late fifties when I joined the group, and seven more were in their forties. They comprised the decision-making body of the group. As they aged, they were not interested in risking a loss of income that might accompany expansion. The lack of young representation allowed the group to stagnate.
- During my nine years as administrator, there were eight different presidents of the group, as well as numerous board position turnovers. This lack of stability was a critical mistake.

- By the late 1980s, physicians were taking home incomes that were above their expectations. This created a false sense of security, as outside competition for patients would soon become a factor.

I don't know if I could have prevented the dissolution of the group or not, but I did learn several important lessons from this experience.

- During my term with the clinic, I followed the advice of my mentors, who used to tell me, "Stay out of the doctors' politics, it's their business, let them decide." I now believe that was faulty advice. A group administrator must be an active advocate involved in the group dynamics. It's a difficult balance, but lobbying support for ideas and voicing opinions on board make-up is critical to the success of the group.
- Avoid the ego of "owning" proposals. If it's good for the business, advocate it for that reason, not because you will be praised for implementing it.
- Recognize when it's time to move on, exhaust your opportunities to change the situation, and go. Staying in a frustrating situation creates a leadership void that hurts both you and the organization.

Mr. Hardy is the manager of CBIZ for Spector & Saulino in Akron, Ohio and was on the American College of Medical Practice Executives board of directors from 1989 to 1992.

Operations

Joseph C. Hutts

PERHAPS THE MOST important message I can convey to aspiring healthcare leaders is that the long-term prosperity of any enterprise is not built on its intermediate successes, but rather on the organization's response to adversity. Every manager/leader needs to understand and embrace this concept, because he or she is certain to experience setbacks during the course of his or her career. How a leader reacts will ultimately determine whether they succeed or fail. I believe that keeping a positive attitude and staying focused on the future are the key strategies for weathering those difficult times.

Healthcare has become a very volatile industry because of the effects of the most significant reimbursement compression in history. The economic foundations of many medical groups, hospitals, and other healthcare enterprises have been badly eroded, precipitating a loss of confidence in the future viability of these institutions. Many of those institutions have begun to unravel, and the pervasive air of uncertainty threatens the existence of others. While this is certainly not a comfortable situation, we believe there is opportunity in this adversity.

Physician practice management (PPM) is only one segment of the healthcare industry that has been severely disrupted by the steep decline in revenues. Some PPMs have exited the business because they could not withstand the financial, social, and political pressures that came with this economic stress.

We are still convinced, however, that PhyCor's founding concepts are sound and that we can add real value to medical groups. We also clearly recognize that we need to adapt to the changing environment and refine our business model if we are to succeed. In that respect, hardship has forced us to reexamine our core business and look for new avenues to improve the performance of physician organizations. Some in healthcare have the mind-set of victims; we believe this adversity can make us stronger if we respond well.

What have we done to overcome the barriers imposed by the changing healthcare environment?

1. We are paring down our affiliated groups to a core of organizations that understand the realities of the environment, and are able and willing to compete in a much different health field.
2. We are not buying assets of the group. Instead, we are joint venturing selected new equipment and services as they are needed to enhance group operations.
3. We are creating programs that truly measure and quantify benchmarks and best practices and are exporting them from group to group.
4. We are using this time of market uncertainty to invest in our infrastructure so that we will be better prepared to grow when the market is ready. We also have identified new areas of growth, particularly in network management that now accounts for almost half of our earnings.

The future seems as bright today as it did 13 years ago when our company was founded. We knew that there would be times of adversity and failure. We could not have known the exact nature of the challenges we would face, but we did espouse a philosophy that we believed would carry us through difficult periods: Winston Churchill once postulated that "First we shape our structures, and afterwards they shape us."

We have always known that we must constantly look for new and better ways to carry out our mission.

Churchill also defined success as going from failure to failure with no loss of enthusiasm. At first glance, that sounds pessimistic but, as you think about it, adversity is a constant part of an organization's life. It is a great lesson for all healthcare leaders.

Mr. Hutts is a cofounder and former chairman and CEO of PhyCor, Inc. in Nashville, Tennessee.

Operations

John G. King, FACHE

I BECAME THE CEO of Legacy Health System in July 1991 and quickly determined that I faced one of management's toughest challenges: restructuring the organization of the management team and making crucial decisions in selecting the persons to lead the organization to higher levels of performance.

To give you some background, two Portland-based delivery systems serving Oregon and southern Washington merged in 1989 to create Legacy Health System. Health Link, made up of four hospitals, served the east and south portions of the greater Portland area. Good Samaritan Medical Center, made up of one hospital and a visiting nurse association (VNA), served the central and west metro Portland area.

Legacy's then CEO unexpectedly died of a heart attack after one year in office.

The board chose me as an outside, impartial leader to move Legacy's mission forward. The board of directors wanted the harmful internal competition between the hospitals within the system redirected for overall improved system performance for the benefit of the community and to improve Legacy's position relative to its two competitors.

Legacy had well-positioned hospitals in the Portland area and operated several outstanding clinical programs recognized as the best in the Northwest. However, Legacy was plagued with overcapacity and internal competition. Legacy had lost market share for three straight years. Costs at Legacy were 10 percent above its two major competitors. In essence, Legacy was in third place behind Kaiser and the Sisters of Providence and losing ground. There was not much time to lose; Legacy needed to change the way it conducted its business.

The first six months after I was hired, we developed a game plan for Legacy designed to improve both cost and quality simultaneously. The Legacy game plan included:

- replacing the existing holding company model with an integrated operating company model to promote "systemness" and integration (the mental model for the operating company was easy to understand—it consisted of one board, one management team, one strategic plan, and one bank account);
- installing a management process called "CQI Legacy" to equip management with a common language and tools to improve the core processes and clinical quality across the system and within the operating units;
- reducing full-time equivalents (FTEs) per occupied bed by 16 percent over a two-year period to reduce costs to competitor levels;
- rationalizing clinical programs across the system and close a downtown, niche hospital;
- merging three of the medical staffs;
- making Legacy the preferred employer in Portland; and
- finding a managed care partner or launch a Legacy-insured HMO in the Oregon market.

My biggest challenge was reshaping the senior management team and picking the right players to implement the game plan. The Legacy senior management team had consisted of 16 persons in 1991. I thought we could do the job better with a smaller team whose members each took on larger responsibilities, so we decided to try it.

The new team was in place about one year after my arrival. The ten members of the team, including myself, consisted of five new faces and five existing executives at Legacy. Three existing Legacy executives took larger positions than the new employees. The team focused on implementing the game plan and on building a cohesive management team that had a system-first attitude. The senior management team envisioned a system of care and an organization integrated in mind and function. Reshaping the management structure, promoting executives to new jobs, and recruiting new blood contributed to the team's success.

The need for change at Legacy was apparent when I arrived, but the organization needed a believable road map for change. Formulating that road map quickly allowed me to take advantage of the "honeymoon period" most new executives enjoy, and I was able overcome resistance within the organization. Board restructuring sent a big message to the organization that aided and supported the implementation of other changes in management and operating process. The board set a good example and made their own changes to meet Legacy's needs.

Legacy enjoyed several successes in the 1990s, including:

- overhauling the governance system, reducing the system board size from 23 to 16 members, and adding more women and minorities to the board;
- reducing case cost by 10 percent;
- merging three medical staffs into one;
- CQI Legacy taking root within the organization and twice winning the Oregon Quality Award;
- receiving the Vanguard Award for promoting women in management;
- consistently being named one of the top ten employers in Oregon;
- increasing market share to premerger levels; and
- improving customer service and employee morale.

An important lesson I learned is that management succession planning pays off. After 30 years as an executive officer, I informed the board in 1997 that I wanted to leave full-time employment in 1999. I inquired if they were interested in an internal successor. Even though the board had brought me in as an outsider in 1991, they strongly believed in 1997 Legacy would benefit from internal promotion.

The board and I formulated an internal succession plan that led to Bob Pallari being named as president in July 1998 and CEO in February 1999.

The board had it right both times. They realized Legacy had different needs in 1991 and 1999. I brought a much-needed new way of thinking and objectivity to Legacy in 1991. Bob Pallari is able to provide continuity to a successful foundation laid in the 1990s by the board, medical, and management leadership.

My biggest error or failure was to put the same effort toward medical leadership as I did toward management leadership. Legacy has very well trained clinicians, whereas management issues needed more attention.

Comparing the past decade at Legacy Health System and the future landscape in healthcare, I realize that it is much more difficult to forge a new management team today. There is a big shortage in management talent to operate and lead the huge integrated systems we have created in the last few years. Addressing management resources is too often an afterthought as organizations merge. Search firms today are desperate for applicants with proven records of accomplishment to fill large system CEO positions. Organizational demands have simply outstripped experienced management talent available, and organizations are not addressing sufficiently their opportunities for growing talent from within.

My advice to boards of trustees and to CEOs is to focus on management development and management succession. Otherwise, the organization's problems will get worse, not better.

Mr. King is the president of John G. King Associates and was the chairman of the American Hospital Association board of trustees in 1998.

Operations

Sara M. Larch, FACMPE

MEDICINE IS ABOUT taking care of people, and I believe physicians, nurses, and other clinical professionals do that very well. The reality is, however, that these individuals cannot fulfill their mission without competent practice support staff and effective business systems to keep an organization financially viable. In my opinion, the primary responsibility of the medical practice executive is to ensure the economic success of the group so that "health caring" can take place.

Most of my career has been spent in practice operations with a significant emphasis on the business office. Over the years, I cannot count the number of times we restructured billing and collection policies, shifted task responsibilities, and overhauled business procedures in order to invigorate group collections. While most of these moves resulted in incremental improvements in our financial performance, none made the kind of impact that I was looking for. It finally dawned on us that our approach to the problems of declining cash flow was backward.

As managed care's grip became tighter and collections declined, we tended to blame the billing process or the staff. We grumbled that we didn't have enough staff, we weren't organized appropriately, or our personnel didn't work very efficiently. Parenthetically, I don't think we were much different than most other medical groups in that respect.

One day, after years of denial, we concluded that collections begin on the front end of the patient encounter, not on the back end in the business office. It was then that we set out to try to reorient ourselves to the imperative that we put more emphasis on getting up-to-date, accurate information when the patient is first seen, and confirming or revising that information each time the patient returns. The task was clear, but changing the mind-set was more difficult.

Intuitively, I felt that we could not improve on front-end performance without investing more money in the registration and appointment scheduling functions. That meant better processes, more qualified staff, and more intensive training. Convincing physicians to spend more money while collections were declining seemed a daunting challenge. I knew that I needed data to support my position, and I set about collecting it. My problem was that I continually looked for the perfect data. I struggled constantly because I couldn't get enough data to satisfy myself. Therefore, I procrastinated in presenting anything to the physician leadership. I had convinced myself that I would only have one or two chances to make my case, and accordingly, I had to have an infallible case.

That, as it turned out, was faulty thinking.

I was able to generate statistics on how many claims had been denied because of inadequate demographic information, lack of proper referrals, and incorrect insurance coverage in some (but not in all) departments. I also knew how much it cost to rework claims. Finally, I knew I had to take a chance and move forward. I presented my case.

I was astonished at how well the sample data was received. With only a few examples, the case for the investment had been made.

The physicians readily agreed that spending money on improving the up-front processes would yield higher dollars at a lower cost. The changes were implemented, and the returns have justified the effort. What did I learn from this experience?

- Good collections do, indeed, begin with registration and appointment scheduling. You must have intelligent and energetic people in those positions. They will save you money in billing costs, save time in the billing office, and will clearly enhance cash flow.
- There is no such thing as perfect data. Don't wait until you have all the data before taking action. Good samples serve the same

purpose and don't take as long to gather. Learn to get comfortable with making decisions based on limited information.

- Benchmark against yourself, not other groups or individual practices. It doesn't hurt to look at national or regional data, but there are too many cultural and operational differences to make those benchmarks universal. Check your own progress regularly. Look for improvement in your operation each time you evaluate your practice's performance. That will be your measure of success—not how someone else is doing.
- Go after the low-hanging fruit first when tackling problems. You learn how to problem solve by taking care of the easy ones first. It will help you refine your process so that the difficult challenges won't overwhelm you.
- Get ahead of the technology curve. Don't wait until someone else perfects a new system or process. Get in the habit of being proactive instead of reactive.
- Remember that operations are at the heart of running a group practice. You must have people with a passion to improve operations, and they must be willing to learn continuously.
- Implement solutions that make sense to your organization, not someone else's.

Finally, never forget that operations are where all the strategies and activities of a medical group come together. A great idea poorly implemented is doomed to fail. The most valuable contribution a medical practice executive can make to his or her organization is to be sure that operating systems and units are efficient, effective, and economically sound.

Ms. Larch is the COO _of University Physicians, Inc., University of Maryland School of Medicine, in Baltimore, Maryland. She is the chair elect of the Medical Group Management Association for 2001 and was president of the_ MGMA _Academic Practice Assembly in 1994._

Operations

Mark R. Neaman, FACHE

MY STORY INVOLVES a ten-year history of our physi-
cian practice group. It illustrates what I would call an error in judgment, but not in decision making. Rather, it was an error of omission
and oversight—making faulty assumptions as opposed to an overt
decision where something went awry.

The story starts in 1985 when managed care was starting to bloom.
Our hospital wanted to get into the managed care business but we
needed to have a doctor group to do it. We went to our physicians
and proposed the idea. At that time physicians were striving for
independence. They didn't want to be owned or employed by a hospital.
So they followed our suggestion and began setting up their own
contracting mechanism for managed care. With our encouragement,
our physicians organized themselves into a group called Physician
Association of the North Shore and began accepting managed care
contracts. They did an excellent job in getting it organized and had
300 physicians onboard. The hospital decided that to protect itself
financially, the operation should be completely turned over to the
doctors. By stepping out of the operation entirely, however, we made
an error of omission.

The philosophy at the time was "If the doctors want to go do it themselves, let them—just don't get entangled in it." As the story goes, the
physician group did some things operationally that they didn't have the
infrastructure to run. They made certain decisions that were not financially supportable. For example, they decided to take in money on a full-

risk, capitated basis, and paying it out fee-for-service. The group didn't have a fee schedule and had not adequately addressed a host of other operational issues. In short, they were undercapitalized. Over a period of three or four years, they ran up a huge bill with the hospital for laboratory and x-ray services. Unfortunately, they couldn't pay their bills.

The next error of omission the hospital made was to say, "We'll try to help you a little bit with the billing part of this." We foolishly stuck our toe into the water but didn't jump in, which just entangled us in their mess. Meanwhile, physicians began crying, "You got us into this, now you've got to get us out of it."

To shorten a long story, the organization dissolved in 1989. It technically went bankrupt.

To the physicians' credit, they did a super job in getting the thing organized, securing the managed care contracts, and bringing more business into the system. The final analysis, however, it that it was just not run well from an infrastructure and operations standpoint.

If I could go back in time, I would address the errors of omission. I would have made a different deal with the physician group from the very start. We would have told them that they had to build sufficient infrastructure to run a group. We would have told them to make the commitment that either the group would secure a couple of million dollars of working capital or to make an agreement with the hospital to provide the necessary capital to make the venture work.

What came out of the collapse of the Physician Association of the North Shore group was the opportunity to form something new. In 1992 we started a new physician practice group called the ENH Medical Group. The hospital is now fully involved in managing and operating what is a very large group. We have 411 physicians as of today in the practice group. It also serves as the managed care contracting vehicle for the nonemployed physicians. So there are another 500 doctors in addition to the 400 employed.

Mr. Neaman is the president and CEO *of Evanston Northwestern Healthcare in Evanston, Illinois and currently serves on the Board of Governors of the American College of Healthcare Executives.*

Operations

Joseph P. Newhouse, Ph.D.

ALMOST 30 YEARS ago, the Rand Corporation offered me the opportunity to become the principal investigator and managing director for a health insurance research project. At the time, neither I nor anyone else could have predicted that the engagement would ultimately consume ten years and over $80 million, and would become one of the most celebrated and influential studies ever conducted in healthcare financing and behavior. Neither could I have known that it would become such an influential element in my career as a healthcare policy analyst, journalist, and teacher.

The purpose of the Rand health insurance experiment was simple. We attempted to address two key questions in healthcare financing. How much more medical care will people use if it is provided free of charge? And what are the consequences for their health? The study eventually enrolled approximately 2,700 families and over 7,700 individuals, but did not include anyone over age 65. We utilized several facilities in California as our behavioral laboratories, including one well-known HMO.

Throughout the 1970s and early 1980s, we diligently went about the task of observing behavior—collecting, classifying, and interpreting data—and drawing conclusions about the relationship of cost, access, and overall health status. In retrospect, we probably over-sampled the poor and undersampled the middle class.

What seemed like a modest undertaking at the time, however, quickly became increasingly more complex as the program expanded through the years.

The results of the experiment have been well documented, and the data is still used today to predict costs in certain populations. In short, we found that the more money people were required to pay, the less healthcare they used. In middle class populations, there did not seem to be any effect on health status. Conversely, in the poorer and sicker populations, there was a marked effect on individual health. This knowledge has been very useful in the structuring of benefits and cost-sharing responsibilities of many Medicaid programs throughout the country.

The message for healthcare leaders does not come from the results of our research, however. Rather, it comes from what we learned by managing the program itself. I had no formal training in management, but prior to taking on the assignment as Principal Investigator for the Rand study, I had managed some other research projects successfully. Because of the smaller size and scope of those activities, it was easy enough to coordinate the research, financing, record keeping, and publication functions of each study. Unfortunately, this experience was inadequate to prepare me for the complexities I was to face in managing the constantly growing activities of the Rand study.

It became apparent early on that we were really embarking on a tridentate pilgrimage:

- creation and operation of a specialized health insurance company, with its functions of recruitment, enrollment, benefits management, financing, and claims processing;
- collection and interpretation of healthcare usage and outcomes data; and
- classification of data and publication of the results for use in the restructuring of healthcare financing and delivery.

As we managed this mushrooming project, it was necessary to employ a deputy director for the study, as well as other individuals/organizations with specialized expertise in performing the tasks of each of these functions. As it turned out, the deputy director added skills, knowledge, and experience that allowed us to maintain control of the process and ultimately bring the Rand experiment to a propitious conclusion. The experience taught us several valuable lessons:

- Managers must clearly understand their own limitations.
- Managers must recognize when they need help, and take steps to obtain that help before the organization gets out of control.
- Managers should seek out associates who bring complementary talents and experience to the organization.
- Communication between managers and associates must be solid so that the expertise and insights of all parties can be combined in the most effective way to reach the goals of the organization.

Dr. Newhouse is a John D. MacArthur Professor of Healthcare Policy and Management at the Harvard Medical School in Boston, Massachusetts and is vice chair of the Medicare Payment Advisory Commission.

Operations

David R. Page, FACHE

SEVERAL YEARS AGO, I assumed a new position as the CEO of a major teaching hospital in the Midwest. Within my first two months with the organization, we were scheduled for our three-year accreditation survey by the Joint Commission on Accreditation of Healthcare Organizations.

Much to our chagrin, when the surveyors arrived for the survey, it was discovered that a recommendation to withdraw our accreditation had been made and that the process could not continue.

Apparently, turnover in management, the lack of a monitoring program, and poor communication with the Joint Commission led to the problem. Because of the severe financial consequences, the impact on our educational programs, and the institutional embarrassment in a competitive marketplace, it was critical that we appeal the sanction and have our accreditation reinstated.

We quickly took stock of the situation and informed the board, management, and our entire staff that there was much to be done to win an appeal and restore our accreditation.

Preparation for the appeal took six months as we:

- engaged outside consultants to help with technical, life, and safety concerns;
- involved management and staff at all levels of the organization to gather, evaluate, and organize data;
- included board members to help us develop the appeal strategy;

128

- completed the foundation for the appeal, studied the material, structured the response, and rehearsed our presentations; and
- videotaped our presentations and critiqued them before traveling to Chicago to make our case.

Our appeal was well received. The verdict was rendered in less than one hour and our accreditation was restored.

I believe we were successful because we disclosed the problem to the board, management, and staff honestly. We also united people in a positive way toward a common goal by involving virtually everyone in the hospital in working on the appeal. Just as importantly, we were thorough and methodical in our approach to problem solving.

This situation, as well as others that I have confronted during my career, confirmed the value of preparation and teamwork in leading a successful healthcare organization.

My advice to healthcare leaders is to face a challenging situation in a positive manner, prepare well, and use all the resources and talents available within the organization. Even the best strategies and programs are doomed to fail without competent teams.

Mr. Page is the president and CEO *of Fairview Health Services in Minneapolis, Minnesota.*

Operations

Sandra W. Reifsteck, R.N., FACMPE

SEVERAL YEARS AGO, results from our patient-satis-
faction surveys at Carle Clinic Association in Urbana, Illinois showed
that our organization's image was beginning to change. Patients were
expressing concerns and dissatisfaction about their individual interactions with physicians. It was a warning signal that we heeded quickly.
With so much publicity about customer service and the growing
pressure to enact a "patient's bill of rights," we knew that we must
take immediate and decisive steps to improve our performance.

In an effort to evaluate our ongoing patient satisfaction scores and
community image awareness results, the administrative/physician
leadership team of the Clinic stratified the data both by individual
physician practice and departmental composite. An assessment of the
data indicated that improvement in our communication with patients
would improve satisfaction as well as the quality of care.

Working with the medical education and marketing departments of
the organization, we embarked on a training program to add patient
communication skills to the educational curriculum for the physicians. We also added a patient complaint telephone line to monitor
our progress.

The commitment of the organization to the improvement of patient satisfaction was accomplished through support from physician
leadership. They encouraged their physician peers to attend educational sessions designed to enhance their communication skills with
patients. As a result, two staff members were trained as facilitators at

the Bayer Institute for Health Care Communication in New Haven, Connecticut. Following the faculty training, a four-hour workshop in basic communication skills was initiated for coaching the medical staff. While not required, each physician was strongly encouraged to attend.

Over a five-year period, other clinicians and support staff were also included in the process.

Today, new physicians and other clinicians are trained annually in the continuing education program and awarded continuing medical education units for participation. Some sessions are split into smaller units of two hours each for rural or off-site locations to accommodate staff unable to attend sessions at the main facility.

The initial workshop targeted clinician/patient communication. Two other courses, "Difficult Clinician Patient Relationships" and "Communication: A Risk Management Tool," were added later.

A key element of the healthcare communication workshops is the interaction among the participants. Video vignettes and structured lectures serve to support these interactions. In this setting, clinicians learn firsthand that good communication skills can enhance the satisfaction of physicians, staff, and patients. They also find that these skills can improve patient outcomes. With these enhanced skills, the clinical staff can also support the best patient care ideals necessary in a growing managed care environment.

What we learned from this initial experience can be used not only by Carle Clinic, but other group practices, medical societies, medical school education, managed care organizations, and malpractice insurance companies as well.

- Support is needed from both physician and top administrative leadership to change organizational culture.
- Communication skills can be learned.
- Physicians and other clinicians typically recognize that technical skills are a given, but what the patient really desires is someone to listen and talk to them as individuals, not cases.
- The majority of malpractice suits are due to misunderstandings between clinicians and the patients. It is reported that the litigation

of one malpractice suit in which no award is granted costs about $150,000. If an award is granted, it is usually quite significant.

- New skill sets to improve communication with patients can reduce telephone complaints and time-consuming routine inquiries from patients after the visit.
- Assisting clinicians in changing negative interactions with patients is more difficult than you can imagine, and it creates a significant amount of negative feedback to the "messenger."
- Nonphysician staff embrace training more readily than physicians, and their behavior is more easily influenced.
- Physicians who develop excellent communication skills are better able to influence/train other physicians than lay trainers.
- The cost in time and dollars of physicians attending communication classes is significant and needs to be considered. The start-up costs of our communication program were borne in the first year, and thereafter our costs were minimal. However, we know that 25 percent of adult patients leave a clinician at some time in their life because of poor communication, and replacing them costs between $450 and $1,500 per patient, depending on geographic location and specialty. This cost should also be factored into any decision to implement a communication program.
- Most participants enter this kind of program feeling that they are excellent communicators and that the program is really for someone else. After completing the program, however, most individuals will be convinced that their communication skills have been enhanced and will be excited about putting their new skills into practice.

One physician evaluating our program called it the best educational program he had ever attended and asked that his entire staff attend. The overall evaluation of the program was very high.

In summary, this was a humbling experience for us in adminis-tration. We learned a tremendous amount from the clinicians and staff about what their days were like in the delivery of quality patient care, and the barriers they faced in communication with patients. We learned that the administrative team must fully understand and support the caregivers' mission and provide whatever training and education is necessary to support their mission.

We recognized that most organizations "slip" at times in their responsibilities to clinicians. However, because of the pervading "patient-first" culture of the Carle Clinic Association, after this experience we understand that communication training must be ongoing for all physicians, physician extenders, and staff. The necessary communication tools are provided to enable the truly trained and instinctive caring culture of this group practice to come through to patients. Now the patient feels first!

Ms. Reifsteck is a Midwest regional consultant for the Bayer Institute for Health Care Communication in Champaign, Illinois and was a board chair of the Medical Group Management Association in 1996.

Operations

Richard M. Scrushy

HEALTHSOUTH HAS GROWN from the acquisition of a single outpatient rehabilitation center in Arkansas in 1984 to being the largest provider of ambulatory surgical, rehabilitative, and diagnostic healthcare services in the world. By having a clear vision of what we wanted to be, we were able to go from being a modest enterprise to transforming the rehabilitation industry in less than two decades. Through dedicated physicians, therapists, management, and support staff, and by having a plan to effectively manage resources, we were able to mature into an international healthcare leader with more than 2,000 facilities in all 50 states, the United Kingdom, Australia, Puerto Rico, and Canada.

As a healthcare company, we recognized early on that any measurable degree of success couldn't be achieved without improving the process of care delivery. We determined that the only way to accomplish that goal was to develop protocols and care paths that would lead to better outcomes, quicker recovery times, and lower costs. That meant we needed to identify the best methods of treating each injury and standardize the use of facilities, equipment, supplies, and staff.

In 1987, we brought together seven physicians and several of our top therapists to discuss the care processes for our most commonly treated illnesses and injuries. We discovered there were 54 diagnoses that consumed 80 percent of our resources, so we began

134

tracking those patient outcomes, resource utilization, and the correlation between the two. Some clinicians were initially resistant to change because they were convinced that their methods were best. However, as we were able to demonstrate equal or better outcomes at lower costs, we achieved buy-in from those physicians and therapists.

Our care team gradually grew to 35 physicians and a like number of therapists. Outcomes for each diagnosis were measured and examined for more than five years. As we were able to demonstrate superior performance, changes were made and the best protocols were adopted. This approach not only had a profound effect on patient care and costs, but it also raised the energy level of our staff and created unity among our facilities.

One example of this program's success can be seen in the transformation of our top diagnosis, back injuries. When we initiated our program, the average back patient was seen more than 30 times during a normal course of treatment. Today, the average number of visits is just over seven. In the late 1980s, the treatment period was somewhere between 10 and 13 weeks; now, it's three to four weeks. The average cost of treatment has dropped from roughly $16,000 per case to the $2,000 to $3,000 range. Most importantly, however, we have seen a marked improvement in the return-to-work rate. Prior to instituting our best practices program, only 10 percent of back patients were returning to their old jobs; that rate is now at 92 percent. The patient has clearly benefited from our protocols, as have employers and society.

HealthSouth has also benefited substantially because of our quality improvement program. By constantly finding better ways to get patients off the healthcare dollar, we have been able to successfully take risks, unlike many of our competitors. This competitive advantage has fueled our prosperity.

We are now competing in a constantly changing healthcare world that rewards ingenuity, resourcefulness, and adaptability. My advice to young entrepreneurs and healthcare executives is to relentlessly search for better ways to deliver care and not be afraid to change when circumstances dictate it. In the fast-paced rehabilitation industry, many companies have failed because they were not on the cusp of change. HealthSouth thrives because we are willing to learn from the mistakes of our competitors and take time to develop protocols that continue to move us into the future.

Mr. Scrushy is the chairman, CEO, and founder of HealthSouth Corporation in Birmingham, Alabama.

Operations

Gordon M. Sprenger, CHE

EARLY IN MY career there was a decision to merge two hospitals in Minneapolis that were located approximately one mile apart. The board of directors believed the two institutions could face the future better together than apart. Their planning, however, did not include a determination as to exactly what that future might bring.

Soon after the merger, however, a major and costly new piece of technology needed to be bought by the new two-hospital system. Its pending acquisition forced the question as to where it should be located. This immediately highlighted the fact that cost savings were not going to be achieved by operating these two hospitals, one mile apart. The broader question of physically consolidating the facilities needed to be addressed.

After carefully reviewing the circumstances surrounding the two institutions, the medical staff voted 100 percent against supporting physical consolidation. There was significant speculation whether the physical consolidation had always been on the agenda by the other institution, but not addressed in the original merger discussion. This allowed distrust to set in. Physicians threatened to take their patients to other locations if the consolidation occurred. While there was significant risk in proceeding with the project, the board and management believed there was equally significant risk in not moving ahead. They doubted it would be possible to maintain two first class institutions located so closely together.

To help settle the matter, I believed it would be helpful to find commonalities between the two sides. I found, for instance, that there was not a difference of opinion in terms of wanting to provide superior patient service in the future. So I focused on what we needed to do to achieve this. It helped narrow the debate to "Could you do that in two facilities a mile apart or better in a consolidated facility?"

By narrowing that focus, it never moved to a vote of no confidence of the CEO or of the board, despite the 100 percent negative vote of the physicians from the campus to be vacated. We decided to deal with the medical leadership up front and made sure that we announced early those appointments that clearly represented the best leadership from both campuses. This also included senior management and department management leadership as well. We engaged the physicians in an extensive planning of the consolidated facilities so they felt they had a thumbprint on it. Because of the close relationship, particularly between the nursing staff and the high-admission physicians, we took several nursing stations in the consolidated facilities and staffed them 100 percent with staff from the closed facility so there was usually a familiar face wherever the physicians would go. The ultimate resolution was that 90 percent of the physicians brought their patients to the new consolidated facility and others in the community joined as a result of the consolidation. Both names were utilized in the identification of the new facility. In addition, designated areas in the new facility retained the names brought forward from the closed facility, such as patient lounge areas named for donors.

We continued to apply our carefully narrowed question of "In the future could we support one consolidated facility and better meet the physicians' and their patients' needs than on two campuses?"

A lot of peripheral issues surfaced but we kept coming back to that focus. We maintained the trust that was needed, emphasizing that there were no hidden agendas outside of what was being stated.

The first important decision was to have the board of directors clearly supporting my vision so that they would not waiver as they were challenged by the different constituencies. Listening was very important so that everyone felt they had an opportunity to place their

position on the table. Engaging the dissidents along with the support-
ers in the planning process of the facilities was key to the ultimate
support of the project. We dealt with the issues ourselves without
hiding behind consultants. We obtained agreement around the vision
of operating a first class facility for our patients and physicians, and
then turned the discussion toward how we were going to achieve that
vision versus disputing the vision itself.

Looking back, I was young in my career and had not experienced
such a situation before. The two boards at the time of the merger decided not to address any changes in the near future because they were
concerned that it could stop the actual merger from occurring. You can
debate whether that was a right or a wrong decision, but in retrospect
I think more discussion could have occurred as to what options were
available. Not using outside consultants had its advantages—it forced
the board, medical staff, and senior management to be in constant
dialogue with each other.

I believe the greatest skill of a leader of an organization is his or her
ability to anticipate the future. It is not that you always have the answer
as to what is coming over the mountain, but that you've positioned
your organization to be nimble and able to respond to whatever the
opportunities or challenges bring. You do this through networking
with other colleagues, reading, carving out thinking time on your own
calendar, listening to local and national thought leaders, and always
anticipating the future and never feeling satisfied with the present.

Mr. Sprenger is the president and CEO *of Allina Health System in
Minnetonka, Minnesota and was chairman of the American Hospital
Association board of trustees in 1996.*

Operations

Alan M. Stoll, FACMPE

WHILE STRATEGIC PLANNING is certainly important, serendipitous events often have just as much of a long-term impact on the organization as the most carefully thought out plan. This was certainly true for the Fallon Clinic during my tenure as its administrative leader.

The story I'm about to share taught me a lesson: keep your eyes open and stay on your toes because you never know when opportunity may strike.

One day in the early 1970s, I received a telephone call from our bank explaining that they were going to begin assessing a monthly service charge on our checking account because the daily check activity had grown much larger than they had expected. We were in a growth phase and, indeed, the volume of activity was expanding. However, we had a long-term relationship with them, and I responded that more activity meant more money flowing through their bank. They were adamant about the fee, and so we decided to look at other banking options.

After a short period of time, we were able to establish a new relationship with a bank that not only didn't assess service fees, but also supplied us with a daily deposit courier, as well as several other services that improved our operating efficiency. In addition, they offered us lower loan rates than our old bank and provided us with financial planning expertise not available in the previous financial institution. Out of adversity, we found opportunity. We were much better off than before, but likely would not have taken the initiative to make a change had it not been for the providential telephone call that day.

An even bigger opportunity presented itself to us a decade later. Again, it was a telephone call that got the ball rolling. This time, it was from the administrator of a small local hospital that was having severe financial difficulties who called the physician president of our group. The facility had been a part of the community for 65 years or so, and we felt that we should try to help if at all possible. It was several miles from the Clinic and was not particularly convenient for our medical staff. However, our physician leadership committed to admitting approximately ten patients per week to the facility. The hospital would make land available to us to purchase on the campus to construct a satellite office.

Over time, however, it became clear that these efforts alone could not save the hospital.

After some brainstorming with the hospital leadership and board, it was decided that a portion of the beds could be converted to rehabilitation beds, which would benefit both the Clinic and hospital. With the participation of a local medical school and a private rehabilitation company, we formed a management company and signed a long-term agreement to manage the facility.

A short time later, a decision was made to make a complete conversion to a comprehensive rehab facility.

We obtained a certificate of need from the state to establish a regional rehabilitation facility in the late 1980s, which we later learned was the first hospital in the nation to undergo a total conversion.

The facility has thrived since that time and was eventually purchased by the management company. Again, a plea for help turned into a major strategic move for the Fallon organization, and became an important part of our service network in later years. This time it was someone else's adversity that became our opportunity.

A few years later, another fortuitous event occurred that had an even greater payoff. The Fallon organization had roughly 150 physicians in the early 1990s, with several locations and our own HMO. Once again, lightning was to strike through the telephone. It was in the form of a call from the administrator of a smaller, competing group of physicians who, with the support of our primary hospital, had just signed an affiliation agreement with Harvard Community Health Plan. This was a blow to us and caused friction with the hospital that was not resolved until we actually acquired the hospital a few years later.

I immediately requested a confidential meeting with the administrator and president of the competing group. They expected me to attempt to persuade them to terminate their affiliation agreement. Instead, I proposed the merger of our two groups. This, of course, was completely unexpected, particularly since their announced agreement with the Harvard Plan. To make a long story short, we ended up consummating the merger, thus adding needed physicians, new locations, and additional primary care capacity. This broadened our network and significantly enhanced our ability to serve the community. It proved to be a spectacular event in the life of the Clinic. Once again, we were able to capitalize on an unexpected opportunity to advance the mission of our organization.

These are only three of the many times we were able to take advantage of the random and unanticipated opportunities through the years to strengthen and grow the size of the Fallon Clinic. There was always uncertainty and danger involved when we seized these opportunities, and any one of them could have been a rattlesnake in disguise waiting to bite us. And while we made some mistakes, far more often these adventures yielded positive results because we were alert to the possibilities . . . and bold enough to take calculated risks.

Mr. Stoll is a principal with TWM *& Affiliates in Worcester, Massachusetts and was the vice president for administration of the Fallon Clinic in Worcester from 1970 to 1997.*

Operations

Michael A. Wilson, CMPE

THE DEAN CLINIC in Madison, Wisconsin was a community healthcare leader long before I assumed the position as its chief administrative officer in 1990. The Clinic had more than a hundred physicians and extenders, and by virtually every measure was a flourishing organization serving its patients well. Nevertheless, because of anticipated competition in the marketplace, Clinic leaders concluded that the group needed to embark on an aggressive growth program. From the day I arrived at Dean, my primary responsibility was to help formulate the expansion plan and lead the growth process.

During the next five years, we added several branch offices, approximately 300 physicians and other caregivers, a myriad of advanced technologies, expanded our own comprehensive health plan, and added a countless number of new patient services. We streamlined operations and reduced overhead, and were able to create many new sources of revenue during that period. It was a very successful time in the Clinic's history. And while I was fortunate enough to play a leading role, our success was really due to the efforts of a very competent management/leadership team.

The success we experienced confirmed my strong belief that organizations thrive through the efforts of what I term as "high performance teams." These teams do not magically appear in an organization; top management must cultivate them. While I inherited a group of talented and committed individuals, they had to become comfortable with my leadership style and approach to problem solving before we could achieve our goal of consistently performing at a high level.

This took almost two years.

The first step in the team-building process was to bring the managers together and involve them in formulating the growth plan. We talked about broad strategies, market impact, an overall business plan, and specific functions such as finance, marketing, physician network development, information systems, partnerships and alliances, and governance. We asked for their input, and then challenged them to define their individual roles in carrying out the plan. This helped create a positive energy and enthusiasm that led to high goals and high expectations. Each manager became vested in the overall outcome and worked diligently on their individual pieces of the plan so that they would not hinder or disappoint other members of the team.

The second step in the process was performance measurement. Together, we set specific goals and developed standards by which we could assess performance. We talked openly about what went right and what went wrong, and did not hesitate to change course when necessary. I should mention that we spent more time talking about what was going right than wrong, which created a comfortable and enjoyable work environment. During this period, we only lost one team member.

We believe that our approach to building a "high performance team" worked for several reasons:

- The positive focus created an atmosphere that encouraged calculated risk taking. It was okay to fail, as long as we learned from each other's mistakes.
- The structure of the team encouraged openness and candor, and a focus on *how* as well as *what* to do.
- We eliminated territoriality and fostered collaboration. Individuals were not put in separate "boxes," but were encouraged to offer ideas and suggestions on any aspect of Clinic operations.
- The solicitation of input from every manager created a sense that the "whole" was greater than the sum of its individual parts.

- We became a knowledge-driven organization, where the team became a repository of information that was accessible to everyone.
- Finally, while there was some individual recognition, the emphasis on team performance mandated that most rewards be based on team achievement.

Effective leaders clearly understand that the success of the organization does not depend on one or two individuals, regardless of their positions, but rather on how well managers, supervisors, staff, and caregivers work together. The high performance team approach creates that much-needed synergy.

Mr. Wilson is the CEO *of Medical Professional Associates of Arizona in Phoenix, Arizona and was the board chair of the Medical Group Management Association in 1998.*

PART III

RELATIONSHIPS

Introduction

POLICIES, PROCESSES, AND people—the essential elements of any business enterprise. We studiously write policies to govern how the organization is to function, we carefully design processes that guide daily operations, and we meticulously select appropriate individuals to carry out our mission. Now we're all set, right? Not exactly. At least that's the view of many distinguished healthcare leaders. Their message seems clear: while organizations can't exist without these fundamental elements, long-term success is probably more dependent upon personal relationships than merely balancing rules, procedures, and personnel. In short, it's the quality of interaction between people that more often determines if the healthcare enterprise simply survives or really thrives.

One needs only to look at a few thriving organizations from diverse fields to understand how vital healthy relationships are to success.

One recent high-profile example is the Los Angeles Lakers professional basketball team. For several years in the late 1990s, most experts concede that the talent level of the players was so high that they should have easily won several NBA titles. However, they never seriously contended for a championship until they brought in a new coach, Phil Jackson, who had a reputation for building strong relationships with his players and blending their diverse talents into a cohesive unit. They won the NBA title in his first year. Nothing had changed in the organization except its leadership.

Another visible success story comes from the transportation industry, where Southwest Airlines managed to revolutionize air travel in the 1990s. While most people believe that SWA has been successful because they are the low-fare carrier, the truth is, they have thrived where others simply survive because of their intracompany and customer relationships. From their unconventional CEO, Herb Kelleher, to their ticket agents, flight attendants, and baggage handlers, they are about teamwork and relationships. If you don't believe it, just fly on Southwest one time and you'll understand that the airline thrives because of the fun and unconventional relationships in its workforce, not to mention its zany relationships with customers. Hidden in the enjoyment of the organization is the superior productivity that leads to first-rate economic performance.

Finally, take a superlative healthcare organization like Virginia Mason Medical Center in Seattle. VMMC has an 80-year history of commendable achievement in delivering high-quality, patient-centered care; clinical innovation; participation in charity and community programs; and individual leadership—all while consistently registering solid financial performance. Why? Because the founders created a culture based on relationships between people. Their underlying foundation is teamwork and communication (i.e., one on one) relationships. Just ask any past or present physician, administrator, or staff member why the enterprise is successful, and they will tell you it's the people: One only needs to take a quick look at their web site to see the embodiment of relationship building, and why Virginia Mason Medical Center thrives in this uncertain healthcare world.

Throughout this book, you will see references to the critical nature of people working with others, whether it be patients, physicians, nurses, boards, superiors, subordinates, administrators, or business and community leaders. The venue or position of the individuals doesn't really matter. What counts is that people are comfortable enough with each other that they can embrace a common goal and work toward it in a harmonious and dedicated manner. That's easily enough said, but how is it really done?

The narratives in this section will be helpful. While each of our author/leaders has a unique story, there are distinctly common themes about how to create and maintain healthy and fruitful relationships. Look for these themes as you read each vignette, and see how you can incorporate the lessons and advice into your daily interactions with others.

Our experts identified nine specific conditions and/or characteristics that seem to form the foundation of flourishing relationships. Because the power of these elements is so vividly demonstrated in each of the narratives, we have included some passages from these stories to properly capture these points. Some of them are quite thought provoking.

COMMUNICATION

"Communication ranks as the most important skill (of an effective leader) . . . Active communication includes the ability to listen and to challenge thinking in order to maximize consensus."
—Eileen O. Hardigan

"It just shows that if you put information out there to bright people, show them the facts without prejudice, and show them the advantages and disadvantages to the institution and to those who serve it, positive results can be achieved."
—Charles C. Lindstrom

HONESTY

"I didn't want to rock the boat. I now know that warning signs cannot be ignored, and that budding problems must be confronted early if the organization is to survive."   —Ann C. McFarland

HUMILITY

"Finally, don't take individual ownership for good ideas. Give credit to others and be generous in your praise for those who participate. It fosters buy-in and trust."   —Warren F. McPherson

LISTENING

"My advice to healthcare leaders is to put away egos and preconceived ideas and ask what others want and need. Don't assume that you know what's best for them.   —Richard L. Clarke

OBJECTIVITY

"Understand what others need . . . listen and counsel, but don't judge."   —Mary Alice Krill

PERSPECTIVE

"I erred in looking at the issue only from my perspective. The individual who carefully considers the other party's dilemma, and deliberates about alternatives or compromises in advance of a confrontation, will be more likely to contribute to a productive dialogue and mutually acceptable solution."   —Paul B. Hofmann

TRUST

"It took years for the medical staff to begin to feel a common bond and to develop a true allegiance to one another. We could have avoided that prolonged period of adjustment if we had taken the proper steps (to build trust) on the front end."   —Barbara B. Watson

TEAMWORK

"In health care, few major problems can be resolved by a single person or autocratic bureaucracy. The interactive dynamics of healthcare delivery and financing are so complex that management strategies must be designed to encourage full participation by the stakeholders."
—C. Duane Dauner

UNDERSTANDING THE DIFFERENCES

"It is very important that you understand the board structure and dynamics, and constantly assess the role of the board."
—Rupert C. Evans, Sr.

"[T]here are innate cultural differences between physicians and hospitals. Joint efforts are tough, at best, due to these differences."
—William F. Jessee

"In business relationships with physicians, leaders need to make a lot of deposits before they can transact a withdrawal."
—David A. Burnett

Stories are a very powerful teaching tool because they give the listener/reader the opportunity to see inside the mind of the storyteller and place him or herself in the shoes of their teacher. From that position, one can vicariously live someone else's experience in order to learn problem-solving techniques or intellectually try alternative strategies without the risk of consequences or failure. This, in turn, enables one to understand the *context* of the lesson so that it can be applied later with a predictable outcome under real-life conditions.

We hope you will be able to relive the following experiences of many successful and respected manager/leaders, and formulate your own database of lessons learned about how to maintain the optimal balance between policies, processes, and people. The overriding message of this section seems to be that balancing these resources doesn't necessarily mean that each one occupies an equal position. On the contrary, these individuals really believe that the people resource is more critical to success than the other two combined. Paraphrasing from a recent Presidential election—*it's the people, stupid!* The leader who heeds this lesson and cultivates healthy relationships should enjoy a long, productive, and satisfying career because his or her organization is likely to be one that has truly managed to thrive.

Relationships

David A. Burnett, M.D.

IN THE EARLY part of my career, I worked at one of our country's major academic medical centers. As frustrating and bureaucratic as they typically are, these institutions are an origin of invaluable resource and benefit for our country. I was lucky to learn from some of the best minds in the world.

I have always been respectful of the remarkable intellectual talent that blends together to make these organizations successful. Oftentimes, as a result of the intellectual capacity and energy that comes from overachievers, these institutions are a remarkable laboratory for the skill sets that are necessary to lead such diverse personalities. However, as a result of consistency, fairness, decisiveness, and communication skills of their leaders—coupled with the practical translation of their culture and values into reality—they can be highly progressive and successful. On the other hand, regardless of the well-founded intentions of those that lead them, should these characteristics not exist, these same organizations can be remarkably dysfunctional and stagnant. The lack of these traits generally causes significant frustration within the organization and, in a number of environments, they are the reason competitors do not consider the academic medical center a threat.

Like all similar academic medical centers, our institution focused on a myriad of responsibilities that supported the multiple missions of the organization, including clinical service, teaching, and research. One of my jobs was to function as the clinical director of our teaching hospital's endoscopy suite. It was a great learning experience filled with daily challenges.

Referrals for endoscopy primarily came from within the institution, mostly from internists. As a rule, stereotyping of personalities is unfair, but as an internist myself, I confess we are a unique breed. We are trained to respond logically to data and to use our instincts and experiences to diagnosis and treat. Moreover, we can be a relatively stubborn bunch.

Consistent with all of the disciplines within medicine, regimens are continually being discovered that improve the outcomes of the care we provide our patients. During my term as director of the suite, it was discovered and well documented that the administration of antibiotic prophylaxis prior to endoscopy was a preferable plan of treatment.

In an effort to be on the cutting edge of enhanced treatment protocols, we sent the word out to referring physicians that patients should arrive with the antibiotic treatment previously administered, consistent with a well-defined plan and the recent findings well documented from the literature.

It became quickly and painfully obvious that many of our referring physicians did not intend to cooperate. They just refused to administer the antibiotic prior to the patient's arrival in the suite. Now, what do you think the problem was?

I have since become a student of management, the change process, leadership, quality improvement, and organizational dynamics. Both through more formal education and through personal development, I have pursued the understanding of human dynamics and the factors that influence behavior. The concept of professionalism has taken on a new meaning for me as a result of my experiences and my studies. I have found that some people are prone to confuse professionalism with directions that are in the best interest of the organization. These are people who are more interested in their autonomy, independence, and base of power than they are in the improved performance of the organization. These are the individuals who make less than optimal team players. Their egos are bigger than the needs of those they serve.

If I had the luxury of being able to relive those years over again, I would respond differently to the issue of antibiotic administration prior to endoscopy. Rather than assuming that I could simply relate the obvious course of action to those referring physicians, I would lay a foundation with them that reflected on the consequences of the treatment plan and their accountability for the outcome. Essentially, I would help the group come to a point where the course of action was their idea because it was the right thing to do for the best outcome of their patient. It does not matter that the course of action be attributed to an individual. What is important is that the outcome brings value and benefit to those we serve. This ultimately brings success to the organization and the reward that we have been a part of a team effort.

In business relationships with physicians, leaders need to make a lot of deposits before they can transact a withdrawal. The process takes time and patience, but it yields the most effective outcome.

Finally, when working with physicians it is important to earn their trust. Over time, always being right or having one's own way is not as important as earning the trust and confidence of those with whom you work. If you lose that trust, it takes ten times the effort and energy to earn it back.

Dr. Burnett is vice president of the University Health System Consortium and director of the Clinical Practice Advancement Center in Chicago, Illinois.

Relationships

Richard L. Clarke, FHFMA

IN THE LATE 1980s, I was the chief financial officer of a hospital-based healthcare system in Colorado. We had two comprehensive acute care hospitals, an ambulatory surgery center, and an HMO. Like many other systems across the country, we were always looking for ways to improve our relationships with physicians and build commitment to our hospital. Unfortunately, while we may have had a good idea for accomplishing just that, our implementation left something to be desired.

Our CEO and management staff decided that we could demonstrate our commitment to the medical staff and gain some reciprocity from them by building an attractive new medical office building and selling shares of the facility to those physicians who occupied it. Another benefit was the enhancement of our financial picture through an off balance sheet transaction.

We talked with some key physicians, received their support, and started the building. As we proceeded with construction, we held meetings with physicians to find occupant/shareholders. Well, in short, we ran into a stone wall, not so much with physicians as with their advisors. These financial advisors wanted rates of return higher than we could accommodate because of potential fraud and abuse violations, and other considerations that we simply could not afford. Because we could not provide the "sweet deal" they required, we could not sell enough shares.

So it was off to Plan B, which entailed retaining title to the building and managing the facility ourselves. To say the least, we did not do a good job of operating it and eventually had to hire a building manager to take over the task.

The project cost us a lot of money and caused estrangement with some physicians. What did we do wrong? Several things. First, we treated the physician community as a homogenous whole. We failed to see the different constituencies and concerns. Second, we thought *we* knew what was best for them, and failed to ask them what *they* wanted and needed. Third, we didn't engage them in the planning process very early in the project. And fourth, we just didn't communicate our message very well. In a nutshell, it seems that we crafted a solution and then began looking for the problem.

If we could have stepped back in time and started over, we would have put together a larger working group that was more representative of our physician constituency. We would have used these individuals to gather, evaluate, and organize data, propose alternative solutions, and communicate the message to the rest of the medical community.

The working group would have also included some practice managers and financial advisors, as well as physicians and hospital staff. This would have built commitment and enthusiasm for the project before we began, and likely would have resulted in better relations, fuller occupancy, and a more positive bottom line for us.

This and other situations that I have encountered in my career have taught me the value of seeking advice from others and listening to what these advisors and constituents are saying.

My advice to healthcare leaders is to put away your egos and preconceived ideas and ask what others want and need. Don't assume that you know what's best for them. Let them tell you, and enter into a dialogue when there are differences in opinion.

No idea or concept is a good one unless those affected think so.

Mr. Clarke is the president of the Healthcare Financial Management Association in Chicago, Illinois.

Relationships

C. Duane Dauner, FACHE

IN 1985, I assumed the position of president and chief executive officer of the California Hospital Association, which would later become the California Association of Hospitals and Health Systems and the California Healthcare Association (CHA).

Upon my arrival, it was obvious that the hospital industry was divided in Sacramento, the state capital. Because of the divergent views, splinter groups, and noncoordination of public policy development, representation, and advocacy, hospitals were not well served in the legislature or with the executive branch. Everyone knew the problem, and the hospitals, through the CHA's board of trustees, were demanding change.

I assessed the situation by interviewing CHA employees, other hospital advocates, key members of the California Assembly and the Senate, administration officials, hospital executives from throughout the state, CHA board members, and a few people I knew who were knowledgeable about the situation.

The comments and advice I received were consistent:

- the conflict and confusion were detrimental to hospitals;
- resources were being wasted;
- the situation made CHA ineffective as the broad statewide hospital association;
- more fragmentation would occur unless definite action was taken to reverse the deteriorating situation;

- defections from CHA would result; and
- hospitals would lose in the legislative and regulatory arenas as competing groups worked against each other.

Several solutions were suggested, including the idea that CHA should exert its leadership in innovative ways to bring together the various hospital interests and form a relationship that promotes unity while also allowing individuality. Further, the establishment of a mechanism or process was suggested to resolve conflicts within the hospital family, whenever possible.

CHA and the regional associations (known at that time as the hospital councils) were the broad-based membership organizations, representing all hospitals. CHA managed the state and federal advocacy while the regional associations managed local/regional advocacy and provided various membership services. The CHA-regional association relationship was restructured and strengthened, building a better association team. This process continued through the 1990s. Today, CHA and the regional associations form a strong, coordinated unit of corporations, expertise, and resources that are consolidated but remain separate with respect to roles and accountabilities.

The other hospital associations and groups were organized in various ways and with different levels of effectiveness. While they wanted to represent the sometimes special interests of specific hospitals, they also realized that hospitals would lose on many key issues unless a unified, coordinated advocacy team was created.

In early 1986, I called a meeting of CHA, the regional associations, and the various hospital groups. We had an open discussion of the issues and problems. Potential solutions were suggested. Additional time was required to build trust and mutual support. With rare exception, all of the individuals wanted to change the situation and were people of good will. We agreed to meet monthly to improve communications, discuss issues of common interest, and explore ways to structure ourselves.

Within three months, a consensus emerged for a clearer, more collaborative relationship among the organizations and lobbyists. A proposal was drafted to formalize an alliance and establish operational protocols.

Less than two months were required for all organizations to endorse the new "Constituency Group" (CG) model. The CG is chaired by the CHA president, with membership from each of the hospital organizations.

The CG meets weekly by conference call and in person as needed. Continuous exchange of information is made and the lobbyists coordinate advocacy strategies to implement consensus on public policy positions.

The process has evolved over the past 14 years and remains effective at producing unity of policy positions, coordinated use of resources, and private resolution of conflicts. As a result, the hospitals and health systems are well served.

In retrospect, I would do some things differently. Since hindsight usually is 20/20, second guessing is a temptation. If it could be redone, there would have been greater involvement of the elected leadership of each organization. Also, the rollout could have been more effective with the members and outside publics. Finally, steps could have been taken to minimize bureaucracy and gamesmanship; however, there is a fine line between universal participation and the extent to which operational protocols can be established in a voluntary arrangement.

However, I have learned the following noteworthy lessons:

- Diversity can produce chaos or strength, depending on how the situation is managed.
- The proper blend of consolidation and individuality can marshal together the strengths of the parts to create a stronger and more effective aggregate critical mass.
- All stakeholders must participate and take ownership of the result.
- Long-term success requires continuous nurturing and hard work from all parties.
- Occasional differences cannot be personalized or allowed to destroy the integrity of the process or the self-discipline required to remain a part of the team.

- Leadership is the intrinsic ability of a person to:
  - create a vision;
  - put life and meaning into the vision;
  - establish goals to achieve the vision; and
  - work with others to help them adopt the vision and buy into its value, take personal ownership of the vision and goals, and exert their own energies and intellect to achieve them.

Such leadership is built on the premise that results are more important than individual glory, and that meaningful progress extends beyond one person.

In healthcare, few major problems can be resolved by a single person or autocratic bureaucracy. The interactive dynamics of healthcare delivery and financing are so complex that management strategies must be designed to encourage full participation by the stakeholders, buy-in to the process, and commitment to the positions and courses of action that are agreed to by the participants.

Value must be measured from two distinct but essential points of view: the position and needs of patients and the public and the requirements of a viable healthcare delivery system and its components.

Four caveats should be kept in mind:

1. People tend to overestimate the impact of a change.
2. People usually underestimate the time and resources required for change to occur.
3. The more universal we become, the more tribal we behave.
4. The more we integrate, the more we differentiate.

Mr. Dauner is president and CEO *of the California Healthcare Association in Sacramento, California and was a member of the American Hospital Association board of trustees from 1992 to 1996.*

Relationships

Rupert M. Evans, Sr., FACHE

THE ERIE FAMILY Health Center is a federally quali-
fied community health center created in 1970 to bring quality medical
care to underserved communities in the city of Chicago.

By the mid-1990s when I joined their management staff, it had
developed a solid medical reputation but had somewhat of a sordid
management history. In fact, prior to my appointment as executive
director, the Center had seen five chief executives in five years and,
because of compliance issues, was on the Federal Watch List.

How was it possible for such a good medical organization to be
so administratively dysfunctional? In short, it suffered from poor
board/management relations.

While attending a medical meeting in Chicago in 1995, I was
approached by the current CEO of the Center and asked if I might
be interested in leaving my military career and becoming her chief
operating officer. I was a native of Chicago, and the prospect of
moving home after 25 years was appealing. I had known "Anne" as
a colleague for a few years and liked and respected her, so I decided to
investigate the opportunity. I found that the Center's reputation was
good and, from all appearances, the staff seemed like a cohesive unit.
I initially interviewed with the entire management team, consisting
of the medical director, director of nursing, director of social services,
director of finance, and director of human resources. After a couple of
weeks I was brought back and interviewed with the board of directors.
A few weeks later, I was offered, and accepted, the position.

Although it was a relatively peaceful time for the Center's operations, it didn't take long for me to realize that there were serious relationship problems within the organization. In fact, in retrospect, I should have realized that the board was waving a red flag when they interviewed me. Typically, boards meet with prospective CEOS, not COOS.

The next red flag was the assignment of duties. I was given direct responsibility for the ongoing construction program, human resources, and operational logistics, but did not have supervisory responsibility for financial or daily operations. It quickly became evident that the finance director was not well organized and was sloppy in his work. I talked with Anne about the situation and told her that I believed I could improve the finances if she gave me authority over the position. She declined. I decided, however, to support her decision and do the best I could with those areas over which I had control.

The final red flag was raised during one of the first board meetings. I was appalled that several middle managers openly debated issues with Anne during the meeting, and the board did not respond to her in a respectful manner. After the meeting, I asked her about the confrontational tone of the meeting and the disrespectful behavior of her subordinates. She genuinely did not see or understand those dynamics and passed the meeting off as typical for the organization. I knew then that there was trouble ahead.

A few months later, on the Sunday before Anne was due to return from vacation, I received a call from the board chair and was asked to come to the office for a meeting at 7:30 p.m. I later learned that some of the board were in another room working out termination arrangements with Anne, while others were asking me to become the interim CEO. I was very uncomfortable because she had hired me, we were friends, and I understood that the board shared some responsibility for her failure as a leader.

I eventually agreed to take the position, but decided that many changes would have to be made in order to restore the organization to administrative health.

I was simultaneously challenged by the opportunity and anxious about the future. The specter of six short-term CEOS hung over the organization like an albatross, and I knew that the high turnover cycle wouldn't be broken until two major tasks were accomplished. First, I needed to understand how the cycle got started and what fueled it. And second, we needed to develop clear channels of authority and responsibility for the board, management, and staff.

It turned out to be a two-year process.

The board was made up of 13 individuals, seven of whom were from the community at large, and six had specific expertise: an attorney, an accountant, an architect, and a banker. While the organization's bylaws set forth lines of authority and rules of conduct for the board, it was clear that they were not being followed. Term limits had been ignored, and over the past few years, the board had begun to seriously micromanage the operations of the Center. I determined that this had happened because of the failures of past CEOs. One failed because he was a clinician with no real business expertise; one had a poor relationship with the medical director and nursing director; one had been promoted from within the ranks and was never accepted by her former peers; and one had a confrontational style. The other failure was due to an attempt by the board to manage the organization by committee.

Once I understood the problem, we began the healing process.

- I first enlisted the support of the medical director, nursing director, and two influential board members, along with interested government officials.
- Then I had a one-on-one conversation with each board member to elicit their assessment and feedback.
- With the help of supportive board members, we developed a strategy for correcting the deficiencies in board/management relations and instituted policies to move us in the right direction.
- We then began using the rules we put in place to rotate some members off the board and add new ones.
- Finally, we engaged an outside consultant to help us with board development, coaching, and recruitment.

The results of our efforts were that:

- we assembled a stable board;
- we improved our financial performance substantially;
- we were taken off the Federal Watch List; and
- we separated the policymaking and operations functions so that management could effectively run the Center.

I learned several important lessons from this experience:

- My due diligence in researching the organization before I took the initial job was inadequate. I saw the Center as the community did and didn't delve into the inner core enough to see the hidden problems.
- Building good relationships with the management team and staff is critical to success in any organization. Had I not secured the support of the medical director and nursing director, I, too, would have been a casualty and the turnover cycle would have continued.
- It is very important that you understand the board structure and dynamics and constantly assess the role of the board. If it begins to infringe on operations, it is crucial that you enlist supportive board members to put the board back on course. Also, don't hesitate to use outside expertise to help if it's necessary.
- In dealing with boards, you must be patient but firm, and you must foster respect between the board and management. Remember that they have ownership in the organization and will be passionate about how it runs. You must diplomatically impress on them that they have limits and that operations are management's territory.

Mr. Evans is the president and CEO *of the Institute for Diversity in Health Management in Chicago, Illinois.*

Relationships

Eileen O. Hardigan, FACMPE

IN 1976 WHEN I began my role as administrator of obstetrics and gynecology, I accepted a very different position from the one I perform today. Perhaps that is why it has kept me motivated and challenged for 24 years. The issues that were most pressing when I began were personnel issues. The organization needed someone with a background in personnel, and, having worked at two other academic institutions in that capacity, I was qualified.

One of the characteristics that appealed to me in the academic medical center was the autonomy of clinical departments. The self-sufficiency facilitated very strong department chairs that were empowered to develop and maintain successful programs in clinical service, education, and research. Although each of these missions competed for finite resources within the department and the school of medicine, the chair had the ability to focus energy and resources within the department to maximize success and, as a consequence, contribute to the success of the school and the university.

Administrators were responsible for managing a medical group practice with the added complexity of integrating education and research. We had responsibility to oversee the staff and resources for the ambulatory and inpatient programs in tandem with supporting the research and education activities of the department. Management of finances and accounting, billing and accounts receivable, budgeting, human resources, and other duties were expected, but to be done within different systems depending on whether it was university, practice, or hospital based. It was an exciting and challenging time.

Given the authority and autonomy of clinical departments, the roles of the department chair and the administrator in the academic medical center were powerful. In 1980 we even created our own 501(c)3 organization to be able to hire our faculty directly and create an appealing fringe benefit package. Opportunities for investing excess revenue provided adequate savings to support future initiatives. Accountability was to the school of medicine through the dean, but our need to work with other specialties was minimal.

The role of the administrator, as well as the department chair, changed radically a few years ago. As a by-product of these changes, we agreed to relinquish the independence of the single-specialty corporation and position the multispecialty organization for a more prominent role in the marketplace. Although potentially threatening, both personally and professionally, it was necessary to move the larger organization forward and to redefine the infrastructure and governance model to improve our chances of being successful for the long term.

Catalysts for change were the demands of managed care contracting, the perceived need to establish a united front with potential business partners, and the logic of pooling departmental resources with others in the organization to optimize investments and reduce expenses.

In retrospect, our expectations have never completely materialized. However, the decision we made was the right one.

The ultimate success of moving from a decentralized system to a centralized group practice model is predicated on effective leadership. As with any organization, ultimate success is largely a function of those who lead, manage, and support staff necessary to accomplish the work. Coordination of customer expectations with strategic position is essential for success. Such coordination is challenging in an academic medical center. Often, leaders are required to align their decisions with political harmony. Realistically, however, it is possible to create a dynamic strategic direction while maintaining smooth operations. It is essential to continue to move forward, while encouraging the complacent to move forward with the group.

Effective leaders today need more than political savvy to take an organization forward. Communication ranks as the most important skill. Also required are skills in effective negotiations, decision making, consensus building, and being change agents. Active communication includes the ability to listen and to challenge thinking in order to maximize consensus and move to a decision. Inability to do this prompts indecisiveness and paralysis within an organization. Unfortunately, not all decisions can be reached through the "democratic process."

Of the many lessons learned, one of the most important is that it is okay for leaders to make mistakes along the way. By making mistakes, we become more knowledgeable for the next encounter and continue to modify our direction toward the goals. We continue to strive to be the ultimate organization.

The journey is not over; there will be more bends and turns in the road. Half of the fun is the ride.

Ms. Hardigan is the administrator of the department of obstetrics and gynecology for the Medical College of Virginia at Virginia Commonwealth University in Richmond, Virginia and was president of the MGMA *Academic Practice Assembly in 1998.*

Relationships

Patrick G. Hays, FACHE

ONE OF THE more challenging efforts of my 30-plus year career at Blue Cross/Blue Shield Association (BCBSA) was undertaking wide-scale cultural change with an in-place management team.

When I first joined BCBSA as CEO in 1995, I was struck by two significant cultural characteristics. First, there was no strategic plan of any shape or form in place, nor had there been one in recent history. Second, there was a prevailing belief in the Chicago and DC Association offices that the individual Blue Cross plans, which actually "own" the Association, somehow worked *for* the BCBSA staff. There was this constant reference to "the field," which was generally interpreted to mean those little folks out there who ran those Plans—multimillion to multibillion dollar Plans—with the real power and critical thinking being at BCBSA.

The effects of these existing problems were measurable. For example, the "Blues" had been losing national market share for 15 consecutive years, yet this didn't seem to be an issue to the BCBSA staff. I was intrigued by the minimal concern about this market share decline among BCBSA staff. I guess it was generally felt to be "their problem, not ours"—in keeping with the attitude of Plans being "the field" while "great thoughts" were the purview of staff in Chicago and Washington.

I needed to figure out what we could do to help the Plans lower medical and administrative costs, improve product offerings, and enhance brand strength to assist them in reversing this market share decline. I decided to tackle the culture problems by using the power of strategic thinking and execution—what later became known as "the strategic framework."

We organized a series of joint weekend retreats for the senior staff of both offices to determine what we at the Association could do to make a difference—to add value—for the Blue Cross and Blue Shield Plans. At the time, there were 69 BCBS plans across America, Puerto Rico, and Canada.

As it turned out, the introduction of strategic thinking into this group of senior staff content experts was difficult and controversial—especially by this person from the "left coast" of California (me). It was difficult for them to believe that they actually could do anything to positively affect the results among the Plans or even that it could be a dimension of their role. The view seemed to be that it was the responsibility of those running the Plans in the field to support the BCBSA staff, not the reverse.

With a lot of hard work and a good deal of pulling and pushing, we began to forge a common vision and arrived at some pretty good ideas. We took those ideas and put them into what was labeled a "strategic framework." It wouldn't have been appropriate to call it a strategic plan, merely a framework from which goals could be developed and measurements could be made as to our progress and contributions.

The next step was to take this very rough draft of the strategic framework to each and every one of the 69 Plans' CEOs. We set up a schedule to meet at hub airports across the country so that every CEO—the "owners"—could preview and react to the ideas.

We got a lot of reaction. Most of it was, "Do you really think you could achieve these items? If so, they could be of great assistance to us."

To get the emerging strategic framework into the formal governance structure, we took it to the board's executive committee for their reaction. They were still getting over their initial surprise at the new interest shown by their Association in even trying to assist them in the marketplace challenges. Mirroring the Plan CEOs' views, there were a lot of questions from the board about the ability of the staff to follow the framework. They were skeptical that any real change would take place.

However, as I sketched my intent to redesign the management incentive plan and tie it to the strategic framework and annual, measurable objectives that would flow from it, the board became convinced that this was a serious plan for real change.

As for how the staff reacted to this proposed incentive change to their bonus plan, you could hear the howls from Washington to Chicago and back again. The historic management incentive program had involved arcane mathematical formulas of artificial precision that related little to observable performance. To propose that senior management be held accountable to standards the board could actually understand was jarring to incumbent staff, to say the least.

To put this in context, I committed to the board that we would live within the BCBSA budget and would not be asking for the historically usual dues increases, given the decline in our Plans' profitability and market share over the past 15 years. This was also met with consternation from the staff, but quickly injected them with fresh financial discipline. At a minimum, it blew away any vestiges of "business as usual." After a good deal of thrashing, however, the Plan was revised, modified, and recommended to the full board.

Nine months after my arrival, at the annual meeting of BCBSA, with virtually all Plan CEOs in attendance, the item took about five minutes on the agenda and was unanimously approved.

Once the board gave its approval, we had the ability and willingness to adapt to our strategic-framework-driven organization. The only exceptions were two senior executives. I had sensed they were becoming saboteurs to the culture shift, so I had to let them go.

In the fall of 1996, the first full cycle since my arrival, we were still struggling to adapt to the changes and had not done particularly well on our objectives in support of this strategic framework. When the lowest bonus payout occurred, which reflected our performance as it should have, it got everyone's attention. People realized their wallets were at risk, which is exactly what I had hoped would happen. I'd have been a little disapppointed if we had hit a bunch of home runs that first cycle and everybody had great bonuses and said this is just like the old days. Instead, some said, "What happened? I haven't had a payout this low in years."

Our response was, "Well folks, you remember those objectives we set and those quarterly reviews that were in the red zone—that's why you didn't get as big a payout as you might have."

One of the things I created to determine bonuses was a value report, which caused a fair amount of pushback from the staff members. They didn't necessarily like their performance being measured against a set of quantitative criteria. Getting them to document for the value report was like pulling teeth the first year.

The second year, I had several people complain that the report takes a lot of staff time that could be used more productively. I told them the value reporting was not going away and that, "You just need to figure out how to get your resources lined up and get it done."

If I had to address the problem again, I might change a few things. Even though I felt it was important to reassure an in-place team of content experts that I wasn't there as a "hatchet man to prune the deadwood," looking back I would have probably replaced a few more of the top 15. Undertaking large scale, multifaceted cultural change with an incumbent management group and a dysfunctional work environment is not for the faint of heart or the impatient.

I can't quibble about our success: the "Blues" are in their fifth straight year of national market share gains—covering one in four Americans—and stronger than ever!

My advice to today's leaders is that strategic thinking and execution is the single most powerful tool at management's disposal. It sets the landscape for accountability, performance measurement, resource deployment, creativity, organizational momentum, and fun.

Mr. Hays was the president and CEO *of Blue Cross/Blue Shield from 1995 to 2000 and currently serves on the Board of Governors of the American College of Healthcare Executives.*

Relationships

Paul B. Hofmann, Dr.P.H., FACHE

As CEO OF a major university hospital, I was pleased that we achieved our budgeted financial objectives. Our previous rate increase was small, and we successfully justified the increase in both written and oral testimony to Blue Cross. Our cost structure and revenue requirements were also thoroughly documented in the budget approved by the boards of both the medical center and the university. In addition, our commitment to demonstrate a clear relationship between the cost of providing patient care and the related charges was consistent with the principles of our long-range financial plan.

Consequently, I was surprised and disturbed when the vice president of medical affairs informed me that the university president had decided to use a portion of the hospital's net income for nonhospital purposes.

The vice president was not willing to appeal the decision because he believed the president's decision was final. However, he did not object to my doing so.

I then made an appointment to see the president. Formerly the dean of the school of theology, the president was highly respected by university employees as well as faculty and students. He and I did not have frequent contact, but we had a good relationship and I genuinely admired his vision and management skills.

The president listened carefully as I explained the reason for wanting to meet with him. He encouraged me to elaborate on my reasons for objecting to the use of hospital funds for an urgently needed university program. I reminded him that the hospital had acted in accordance with a budget and financial plan formally adopted by the governing bodies of both the medical center and the university. Furthermore, our rate increase was based on the need to generate sufficient revenue to support the hospital's operating and capital requirements. Not only within the institution, but also publicly, we had stated consistently that patient charges and costs would be fully aligned. As diplomatically as possible, I suggested his intended action to appropriate a portion of hospital income would violate this repeatedly cited principle.

Quietly but firmly, he asked me if I thought he would be acting unethically. Given his background as a theologian and my deep admiration for him, I hesitated before responding. I replied that he certainly was not intentionally taking an unethical action, but his decision would compromise my role as the hospital's CEO. He then asked what I would do if I were in his position. I admitted that I did not have a solution. He expressed regret about the circumstances and thanked me for my candor.

That evening, I spoke with my wife and evaluated my options. One alternative was to resign, in which case I would need to decide whether to make my reason for doing so public, and to consider the repercussions for the president, the university, the hospital, and myself. After extensive deliberation, I decided against resignation. Instead, I wrote a lengthy letter to the president in which I expressed my respect for him, reiterated my objections to his decision, and proposed that he formally commit to taking the hospital's funds only as a loan and to stipulate repayment within 24 to 36 months. He subsequently agreed in writing.

Early in my career, one of my mentors suggested that an ultimatum should never be issued to force a contentious decision unless the petitioner is prepared to have the ultimatum accepted. Right or wrong, I was not prepared to tell the president I would resign if he did not reverse his decision. I anticipated that he had conscientiously searched for other funding alternatives without success, and would feel compelled to use the hospital's funds even if I threatened to resign. Consequently, what value would have been achieved by my resignation? The president would have proceeded with his decision, my family would have been disrupted, and, immodestly, I did not believe the hospital would have been better off without my presence. I had given thought to resigning both before and after my meeting with the president, and perhaps my reasons for not resigning constituted a convenient rationalization.

Nonetheless, I benefited from the experience. I learned that an emotionally wrenching dilemma cannot always be resolved to everyone's satisfaction, even when the participants are intending to act properly.

In retrospect, I would have approached the problem in the same way with one exception. It would have been helpful if I had given more thought about the president's situation before meeting with him. Instead, I prepared for the discussion solely by mentally listing all the reasons why his decision was objectionable, giving no consideration to potential compromises until after our meeting. Fortunately, the ultimate outcome was palatable, but I erred in looking at the issue only from my perspective.

Inevitably, there will be times when competent people argue passionately in defense of their particular position. However, the individual who carefully considers the other party's dilemma, and deliberates about alternatives or compromises in advance of a confrontation, will be more likely to contribute to a productive dialogue and a mutually acceptable solution.

Dr. Hofmann is the president of the Hofmann Healthcare Group in San Francisco, California.

Relationships

William F. Jessee, M.D., CMPE

A NUMBER OF challenging events, both professionally and personally, have formed the foundation for my leadership style. One of the professional experiences that stands out as particularly challenging, and even uncomfortable at times, was during a period when I was the acting chief medical officer of a rather large hospital system.

In the early days of the Clinton administration's efforts to promote reform in our country's healthcare system, the state in which this system was located enacted legislation that encouraged the development of large integrated systems to compete for market share—or so we thought.

In response, three large hospital systems in our area formed a joint venture to develop a statewide, integrated system of care. My task as acting chief medical officer was to develop the provider network for the system.

We spent almost 18 months deciding on governance. At best, it was a difficult challenge because each system was more interested in protecting their market share and maintaining control than they were in creating a system that served a market that was looking for providers to assume risk. Regardless, we finalized the plan and we created a new not-for-profit organization with a 20-member board of directors. The three partner systems split the board appointments 40/40/20 in accordance with their financial commitment to capitalize the new network.

It was obvious early on that without significant physician participation, the network would not be successful. I've noticed that physicians are not very enthusiastic participants when they do not feel they are full partners with the ability to influence the strategic direction of the organization. I recall hearing something like this from the physicians: "If we aren't equal players, we won't play." And they meant it. Accordingly, physicians (selected by each system) were appointed to half of the board seats.

Shortly thereafter, with the endorsement and support of the most powerful hospital system's CEO, I was appointed chief executive officer of the new network. The physicians insisted that they wanted to contribute money to the project. They proposed that the enterprise be for-profit so that they could be part owners. Their logic was that they would not truly be equal partners unless they had money on the table, along with the hospitals. But the hospitals, equating money with control, insisted that they provide 100 percent of the funding and that the network be not-for-profit.

Following several months of work, we had 1,300 participating physicians in the network. It took long hours each day and hard work to build the trust and relationships needed to convince them to contract with a new, unproven entity that was not yet able to bring them business. But those were the days when the fear of being overpowered by a managed care plan provided the catalyst to be a player with a network you could help direct and control.

I learned a lot about the thought processes of hospital administrators during the journey. For example, I remember being surprised that the hospitals, which were also owners, would not give favorable discounts to our network because we offered no patient volume. They could never get past the idea of making money from filled beds, as opposed to making money from premium income, and keeping people healthy enough to stay *out* of hospital beds. The logic continues to fail me today.

Friction between the owner hospitals and the physicians increased as the hospital system began to feel a loss of control over "their" network. I remember being asked by the powerful hospital administrator that had endorsed my appointment as CEO to clarify whether my loyalty was to the hospital or to the network. It never occurred to me that my energy and loyalty would be anywhere except to the organization for whom I worked (the network), and to the board of that organization.

As the loss of control concerns by the hospitals increased, they covertly developed a strategy to regain command. Essentially, they incorporated another new organization and created a strategy to develop regional charters rather than a single statewide program.

All of this activity became moot when the state replaced the reform legislation the next year. The network was dissolved shortly thereafter.

There were abundant lessons that I learned from this work, but five points really stand out as most significant.

- First, in creating any new program, it's important to take the time to develop a viable organizational design and get the support of the stakeholders. Without prospective agreement on the design, operational effectiveness is virtually impossible. In retrospect, our design was a fragile political compromise and was destined to fail.
- Second, make sure there are properly aligned incentives among the owners, governance structure, and management. Without that alignment, you're sure to fail.
- Third, spend as much time as it takes to ensure clarity of organizational purpose and strategic objectives before you take off on operational implementation. To assume everyone is on the same page without buy-in on explicit goals, objectives, and a clear vision of the future can be dangerous.
- Fourth, there are innate cultural differences between physicians and hospitals. Joint efforts are tough, at best, due to these differences. Nevertheless, they can still be successful if sufficient time is taken to perform the front-end planning.
- Lastly, physicians and hospital administrators do not think alike. I'm not saying one party is right or wrong or good or bad. But integrated systems that are the most successful are those where

these differences are acknowledged and where communications, candor, honesty, and trust are the foundations for working relationships. Ultimately, those organizations that thrive maintain a passion that promulgates the good of the organization and benefits those they serve.

Dr. Jessee is the president and CEO *of the Medical Group Management Association in Englewood, Colorado.*

Relationships

Mary Alice Krill, Ph.D., FACMPE

THE MOST SIGNIFICANT situation I had to deal with during my career is perhaps the most difficult one that can confront a manager/leader. While it is commonplace, it is a problem that is often hidden and, when revealed, is typically ignored.

The situation involved a female employee who was very bright and effective in her work as a specialist in designing survey documents. The data was analyzed and summarized to determine trends that would be helpful to administrators in evaluating the performance of their individual group practices. After an initial record of being on time for work and making significant contributions toward new directions in the collection and reporting of data, she began arriving late for work and exhibiting low productivity.

As a result of all this, I asked her to come into my office to discuss these problems and discovered that she was being abused by her husband. She was in constant fear of what he might do next. In addition, she was pressed to arrange her schedule so that her little boy was never alone with him. She tried to leave, but was threatened by him in such a way that she had decided just to try to avoid any confrontation.

I told her that I understood how difficult it must be and to do the best she could about getting her boy to school and arriving on time for her work. She agreed to work every lunch hour to try to make up the time.

I did not share this problem with my supervisor or others in the office in order to provide some semblance of privacy for the employee. However, one day not long after I had met with her, she was called into my supervisor's office and told if she were late one more time she would lose her job. Obviously, my supervisor had been aware of her tardiness for some time.

I knew that one of my other employees happened to have a significant amount of experience in assisting women who had been abused. I suggested that we ask this employee for her assistance. She offered to help by making an appointment for this woman with SAFE HOUSE, an organization that provides counseling and shelter to abused women. I was eventually able to argue for retaining the troubled employee, but the work atmosphere was a bit strained.

On my last day of work before I retired, the office held a good-bye party. I received a gift from the employee I had supported. The card said: "When you're gone, I'm gone." In talking with friends later, I heard she was terminated the following week.

In retrospect, I probably should have solved the problem differently by attempting to gain top management's support in making an effort to work out a mutually agreed upon solution. Unfortunately, I was convinced top management would not share my compassion for this person. I will never know. At least my effort to keep this woman in her position might have had some promise if I had given my superior an opportunity to feel some ownership in the solution.

Dr. Krill was the director of the Center for Research in Ambulatory Healthcare Administration in Englewood, Colorado from 1978 to 1995.

Relationships

Charles C. Lindstrom, LCHE

A MEMORABLE STRATEGIC problem occurred when our board received a letter from an investor-owned system asking to buy our hospital.

Our board chairman received that letter, fielded telephone calls, and hosted visits from representatives of the investor-owned company. He really wanted to join this system, but he did not want to share all of the details of the deal with us. He simply paraphrased some of the deal in a typewritten summary, which led us to suspect something might be going on. We knew that he was really certain about accepting the proposal; we were far less certain. We weren't necessarily against it; we just had a lot of questions about it.

Meanwhile, the investor-owned company wined and dined our physicians, literally and figuratively. Accordingly, the medical staff developed a strong appetite to rush into the sale.

To take back some control in making this decision, we gathered the facts. We gained as much information as we possibly could about the issue and about the company. We visited their headquarters, we visited with their hospitals in this region, and we visited with CEOs of hospitals that were acquired into their system.

We discussed the matter with our medical staff at every conceivable opportunity to make sure we understood their viewpoints and interests. We wanted to make sure that they knew all the facts and we wanted to hear their thinking. We have a large hospital board, which has numerous committees, and we discussed it at every committee meeting. "Where two or more were gathered" we talked about it.

After a relatively brief period of time, we developed a report. Being as fair as possible, the report listed advantages and disadvantages of the proposal. We prepared it as if the chairman of that investor-owned company was sitting in the front row. It was vital that the report be fair and honest.

First we presented our report to the executive committee of our board and then our board of directors. In both cases our chairman, who is not a member of the executive committee, was present. There was a good, complete, and lengthy discussion where we asked everybody to comment.

At the vote of the executive committee and then at the board of directors, the only person that did not vote for the sale was the chairman. It was otherwise unanimous, including the doctors.

In retrospect, during the three to four months when the purchase was being considered, we did a good job in putting the facts out. We were not trying to prevent the purchase, we just wanted to make sure any decision was good for the health of our organization in the future.

Looking back, I learned that it was wise to stress impartiality when facing a task of developing pros and cons. I learned that I had to put aside the preconceived ideas that I had held.

If I had to share advice to other healthcare leaders, I'd tell them to think clearly and carefully about all the issues with an open mind. Gather facts impartially. Present everything, both the positive and negative. Make sure it is as fair as it can be and then communicate the issues without prejudice and without harming any other relationships.

The approach we tried to take was one that was a little more thoughtful and scholarly: "Let's really study it and look at the facts." In going into the meeting, I thought it had a two-thirds, one-third chance in getting through the executive committee and about 50–50 for the medical staff. To have it go practically unanimous was kind of rewarding. It just shows that if you put information out there to bright people, show them the facts without prejudice, and show them the advantages and disadvantages to the institution and to those who serve it, positive results can be achieved.

At the end of the day when all things were done, board members and physicians said, "This was a real education for us." It made working together with the board and medical staff of the hospital more positive. We all felt closer afterwards.

Mr. Lindstrom was the president and CEO *of St. Luke's Health System in Kansas City, Missouri from 1966 to 1995.*

Relationships

Ann C. McFarland, FACMPE

PERHAPS THE SINGLE most dominant trend of the 1990s was the rush to create integrated networks of physicians and hospitals. The urgency that drove this strategy was the need to effectively compete in the burgeoning managed care milieu. My experience involves one such venture.

Two prominent hospitals in Southern California joined forces in 1993 to create a three-tiered structure that they believed would serve patients more efficiently, cut costs, and ensure long-term viability for both hospitals in a highly competitive marketplace.

Physicians were open to the venture because they were fearful of being dominated by health plans.

The system included a management services organization (MSO), an independent practice association (IPA), and a foundation model group practice.

I was a medical practice executive familiar with both hospitals and was subsequently offered an opportunity to lead one of the three newly created organizations. I served as chief executive of the MSO and was on the governing board of the subsidiary that owned the IPA management company and MSO.

The theory was that these three organizations (MSO, foundation model group practice, and IPA) could align the interests of physicians, hospitals, payers, and the consumer by giving each of them a voice in how business was conducted. Unfortunately, this never materialized. The MSO was developed to provide billing and accounts receivable services, group purchasing, and systems management. It also became the employer for all the support staff of the medical practices. This was thought to be a positive way to turn each practice/group into productive "clinical care sites."

A 10,000-member IPA was purchased by the system from a sole physician owner to establish market presence. Eventually, the IPA grew to 60,000 members. The foundation group practice did not exist and had to be constructed from the ground up.

Within 18 months, three more hospitals were added to the mix, as well as many new physicians. I saw warning signs as these organizations were being developed, but I wanted so much for them to succeed that I ignored the signals, kept silent, and continued to build the supporting elements that I believed would lead to success.

The ultimate failure of this venture was not because it was a bad strategy, but rather because of poor design and implementation. Proper relationships between the three were not formed, communication between the parties was inadequate, and too much gamesmanship developed between hospitals. Physician interests were all but ignored. This, of course, caused suspicion, mistrust, and financial stagnation.

Over a period of three years or so, the board of trustees of the system became disenchanted with the poor economic performance of the enterprise. Management of all three units was given a year to fix the financial problems and generate operating profits. Failure to do so would result in dissolution of the venture. These objectives were not met, and the MSO organization was collapsed in 1997, the IPA management company was dissolved in 1998, and the IPA was sold in 1999.

The foundation group practice continues today; however, its future remains uncertain as an organization.

During this time there never appeared to be acknowledgement by the system that lack of a coordinated, integrated management structure within the physician organizations might be an issue to the overall financial viability of the three organizations.

In spite of these obvious problems, there were some positive effects of the endeavor for physicians:

- Operating efficiencies were realized in virtually every medical practice.
- Staffing was reduced, purchasing programs produced savings, billing processes were streamlined, and collections were improved.
- Sophisticated financial systems were installed, enabling physicians and management to more clearly evaluate practice economics.
- Compliance programs were implemented for all practices.
- Health plan credentialing was simplified and improved.
- Contract negotiation was enhanced, yielding better reimbursements for physicians.
- Practices began spending more time concentrating on clinical issues than economic ones.

Unfortunately, these positive developments were overshadowed by the negative politics and lack of a proper organizational foundation:

- Contrary to its original intent, the board of trustees never included any physician organization representatives. All trustees came from the hospital governing boards of the affiliated hospitals.
- Each component of the triad had separate administrators, rather than one individual to communicate with all parties.
- The MSO, IPA, and foundation had separate boards and pursued their own interests. Additionally, there was no physician representation on the MSO board.
- Because the contributions of each hospital to the capitalization of the entire enterprise were not equal, animosity developed between them and competition replaced cooperation.
- There were too few physicians at too many sites.
- In attempting to build the organizations, political outcome was considered rather than whether or not it made economic sense. Too many bad arrangements were made for political reasons.
- The arrangements made with physicians were too generous and lacked incentives for physicians to work. Ultimately, they collapsed under their own economic weight.

What did I learn from this experience?

- I was seduced by the opportunity to lead a bigger organization and did not ask the necessary questions before taking the job. I knew that they should be asked, but subconsciously, I didn't want to hear the answers. The tough questions must always be asked, regardless of the consequences.
- I did not speak up when I saw the selfishness and competition among the hospitals and when they did not live up to the promises made to include all stakeholders in decision making. I didn't want to rock the boat. I now know that warning signs cannot be ignored and that budding problems must be confronted early if the organization is to survive.
- I failed to address the mixed messages, lack of communication, and stretching of values for so long that I became part of the problem. I strongly believe that the values of the enterprise and the individual must closely match. If they don't, you must make the difficult choice of leaving the organization. You can't sacrifice those values for professional gain.
- Relationships drive organizations. If not properly cultivated, the organization will perform poorly and may ultimately fail.

Ms. McFarland is a principal with HealthCare Management Associates in San Clemente, California. She was president of the Medical Group Management Association Integrated Healthcare Practice Society in 1997 and served on the board of the American College of Medical Practice Executives from 1996 to 1999.

Relationships

Warren F. McPherson, M.D.

EACH OF US is shaped by life events, people, the environment, our personal interests . . . and even random circumstances. These influences give us our rather unique perspective of the world and provide the framework for how we live, work, and interact with others. It is vital that we remember this when building and leading organizations because these different viewpoints will invariably affect the organization's decisions, operations, and its ultimate success or failure.

I believe that people and relationships—not strategy—generally drive organizations. The best strategies and tactics often fail when working relationships are less than optimal. Consequently, the healthcare leader's most important task is to mold diverse interests into a cohesive unit and to build strong relationships that can transcend those differences.

It was late in my medical career when it hit home that honest and capable individuals could have legitimate differences of opinion without there being a right or wrong side of an issue.

I, like all physicians, was trained in the "scientific model," where facts are gathered and presented logically and rationally. Once these facts are organized and analyzed, they should lead all observers to the same single conclusion. I found out rather abruptly while working on an MBA that business and commerce don't always lend themselves to the scientific approach, and that the "business model" stresses collaboration and negotiation. The approach not only tolerates diverse opinions, but actually encourages independent thought in problem solving. The business model is grounded on the premise that the free expression of alternate opinions leads to better decisions. It's a lesson that has served me well throughout my career as a physician and organizational leader/administrator.

State Volunteer Mutual Insurance Company (SVMIC) was one of the many physician-directed enterprises that developed as a result of the malpractice insurance crisis in the mid-1970s. Because I had an interest in financial affairs, I was asked to serve on the investments committee of the company in the early 1980s. It was in this venue that I first began to practice the art of collaboration and consensus building.

A few years later I was elected to the board of SVMIC and was fortunate enough to become its chairman in 1994. This experience strongly reinforced my belief that cooperation and consensus is an organizational imperative, and that it starts with one-on-one relationships. I have found that these much-needed relationships are built on honesty, sincerity, and respect for the opinions of each member of the group.

Through my leadership involvement in SVMIC, I became engaged with the Physician Insurers Association of America (PIAA), a trade association of physician-directed malpractice insurance companies. While the governance and organizational issues for PIAA have been different than for SVMIC, the basic principles remain the same: find ways to take independent enterprises, with diverse goals and strategies, and mold them into an organization that can effectively represent their collective interests. By allowing constituents to express their opinions without restraint and fostering collaboration between members, our results are always better.

The formation and development of our community physician organization, the Stones River Regional IPA, has also provided confirmation that organizations rise or fall on the leadership's ability to get members to subordinate their individual short-term self-interests to the best long-term interests of the group as a whole. It takes trust and respect to accomplish that task, and it only happens through flexibility and dialog among the parties. Many such organizations have failed because they could not achieve this collaboration. Ours has succeeded because we have.

Different types of organizations . . . with completely different missions and widely disparate constituent bodies . . . why do they all thrive? I'm convinced that they're successful because they have been able to effectively bring their constituents to common ground and united action through their emphasis on building relationships and fostering collaboration. The leadership of these ventures seem to understand and heed the principles and realities of organizational behavior and use them as a guide to advancing their missions.

Those principles and realities are as follows:

- There will always be differences between the wishes, desires, and needs of organizational members and staff. Respect those differences and seek to understand them.
- Use the mission of the organization to guide policy, strategy, and tactical discussions. If the focus is on the mission, it will be easier to bring constituents to a consensus.
- Always look for a connection between conflicting points of view, and use it as a vehicle for bringing the parties together.
- Introduce concepts to individual decision makers before meetings are held to discuss or vote on specific issues. It gives each individual a chance to think through alternatives. At the meeting, let strategies and logistics "bubble up" from the discussion. It will always lead to more consensus and better decisions.
- Finally, don't take individual ownership for good ideas. Give credit to others and be generous in your praise for those who participate. It fosters buy-in and trust.

Dr. McPherson is a practicing physician with Mid State Neurosurgery and CEO of the Stones River Regional IPA in Murfreesboro, Tennessee. He is the current board chair of the State Volunteer Mutual Insurance Company and was board chair of the Physician Insurers Association of America in 2000.

Relationships

Barbara B. Watson, FACMPE

THE LAST DECADE of the 20th century was clearly the era of practice consolidations, alliances, and integration. It was during this "urge to merge" period that I learned a great lesson about the importance of building relationships and creating a common culture.

I was the chief administrative officer of a 12-physician orthopedic practice in a very competitive marketplace. We had three offices located strategically in the community and a nice variety of subspecialties.

We were prosperous and satisfied, but believed that we needed to grow to secure our future. It seemed obvious to us that the most effective path to growth was through a merger with other orthopedic surgeons in the area. There was another group in town that was situated in various locations that were complementary to ours. They were roughly the same size as we were, and putting the two groups together made excellent strategic sense. It would end up being a groundbreaking merger, creating one of the largest orthopedic practices in America at the time.

We engaged the proper legal and financial consultants to help guide us through the logistical steps of merging, and held countless meetings with our counterparts to talk about operational and financial details. We considered the emotional toll on our employees, and engaged an employee assistance plan (EAP) to meet with our employees to explore the effects of change.

After a great deal of investigation, everyone in both groups agreed that the merger made sense. We decided that we would eventually construct a large building to house our major downtown clinical and business operations, but agreed that we would keep three separate downtown offices open until the new facility could be constructed.

The process took four years. A few physicians from both groups were immediately relocated so that we could put subspecialists together for patient convenience. Spine surgeons occupied one office; joint and hand surgeons were in another facility; and pediatric orthopedists in still another one. General orthopedic surgeons were in more than one location, including our three satellite offices.

We recognized early that we needed to work hard to create a comfortable environment for the merged support staffs. Accordingly, we focused on them, and took for granted that physicians would be able to adjust without too much orientation. That was a big mistake. We assumed that since most physicians were intimately involved in the negotiations, and consequently voted to proceed with the merger, that they would be at ease enough to adapt to the new organization without outside help.

It surprised us that this was not a correct assumption.

While signs of discontent showed in the behavior of a number of the physicians, one physician seemed more discontented than the others did. He complained about virtually every administrative procedure, staff members, facilities, and everything else, including the administration. For awhile, we passed him off as a malcontent and troublemaker. Nothing could have been further from the truth.

At our quarterly meeting, the director of our employee assistance program talked with me in general about their observations on the effects of the merger (we had made their services available to all employees, but specifically had engaged them to counsel employees with merger-related anxieties). They shared with us that they had a consult with one of the physician staff members. The physician who had been acting out his distrust and hostility had consulted her, and ultimately gave his permission to discuss his feelings with our physician leadership and me. There was really a very simple explanation for his anger—he felt a profound sense of loss. The group that he had grown up in was gone. He was now only one of 27 voices in policymaking. He was fatigued and frustrated with the changes in his professional life and ultimately it was affecting his personal life. Armed with that knowledge, we were able to eventually build a trusting one-on-one relationship with him. He became one of the best team members in the group. We now had a clearer understanding of physician needs in a changing environment.

What we learned from this merger was that relationship-building in the molding of a new culture is just as important as daily operational logistics or income distribution issues. It took years for the medical staff to begin to feel a common bond and to develop a true allegiance to one another. We could have avoided that prolonged period of adjustment if we had taken the proper steps on the front end. What should we have done?

- We should have engaged a psychologist/consultant to handle the relationship-building process between physicians, just as we did for other clinical and administrative employees.
- We in administration should have been more proactive in trying to cultivate relationships with the new physicians by listening more intently to their issues and being more visible at all locations. From this experience we developed a physician orientation program for future physicians.
- We should have recognized that different and separate relationship-building strategies would be necessary for physicians.
- We should have instilled a stronger sense of pride that we were breaking new ground and creating a visionary new type of group.

It is clear to me now that economic prosperity can be created by paying attention to the business details. Those organizations that *really* flourish, however, focus on communication and relationships. They realize that people, not systems, create excellence.

Ms. Watson retired in 1997 as chief administrative officer for Charlotte Orthopedic Specialists, Inc. in Charlotte, North Carolina. She was president of the Medical Group Management Association in 1995 and president of the American College of Medical Practice Executives in 1994.

PART IV

CAREERS

Introduction

CAREERS ARE LIKE fingerprints—no two are exactly alike. They may appear to be the same on the surface, but it only takes a little closer look to see that each career, like a fingerprint, has its own unique design. Because every one of us has a different combination of talents, personality, educational achievement, ambition, environmental background, work experience, and aspirations, it only makes sense that every career will take at least a slightly different path.

If that's so, what can we learn from the careers of other people? Plenty. While we can't create the exact pattern of someone else's career, we *can* learn things from the experiences of other leaders that will help us craft our own personal success and career satisfaction. This section of *Trials to Triumphs* is an illuminating looks at the careers of several very prominent healthcare leaders. They have been very candid in speaking about their struggles, failures, insecurities, mistakes, and ultimate triumphs.

Why do very talented people sometimes fail, and how do seemingly average individuals sometimes attain high levels of achievement? And, what are the implications for us? According to our contributors, the answer is relatively simple: having talent is a good start, but there are many other critical factors that affect our career progression and success, some controllable and others the result of mere circumstance. Not a very comforting thought, is it?

Their message to us is that we can only apply our talents honestly and conscientiously, and accept the fact that there is an element of randomness that affects us all. Such factors as timing, compatibility with the organization, and environmental influences can enhance or redirect our careers. Actually, this is good news because all of us are not blessed with the same levels of intellect, skills, or charisma, and yet it's still possible for virtually all of us to fashion a satisfying and thriving career.

What this tells us is that there is no single formula for career success. On the following pages, we learn from prominent leaders in all walks of life that we create the best chance for a productive and fulfilling career by being ourselves rather than trying to emulate someone else. They agree that careers are as erratic as the people who manage them, and very often there isn't a predictable or neat pattern. In fact, careers are typically haphazard and messy. These distinguished individuals also contend that this is not a bad thing. If we all followed some magical path to career success, there would be a lot less spontaneity, innovation, or stimulation. There is an energy that is created by uncertainty that's vital to our sense of well being and achievement.

The implication seems to be "relax and enjoy the journey."

Perhaps we can grudgingly accept the fact that there is no magic formula for ensuring career success. But there must be some basic tenets that amplify our chances of shaping a thriving, meaningful, and rewarding career. Luckily, our prominent leaders can offer some useful pearls for improving career potential. Look for them as your read each commentary, and think about how you can use them as you write your own success story.

ON PLANNING YOUR CAREER

"You don't."   —David M. Lawrence

ON KNOWING WHEN IT'S TIME TO MAKE A CAREER CHANGE

"When you sense that you're becoming more about maintenance than innovation, it's time to look for a new opportunity."

—Thomas C. Royer

ON SKILL SETS NECESSARY TO BE A GOOD LEADER

"Respect for the work of others . . . team orientation . . . confidence."
—Frederick J. Wenzel

ON HOW TO BE A SUCCESSFUL LEADER

"You must be interested in something bigger than yourself."
—Donald M. Berwick

ON THE UPSIDE OF MAKING A CAREER CHANGE

"It affords opportunities for increased responsibility, more income, and a chance to expand your skills and knowledge."
—Sherry A. Gentry

ON DEALING WITH TERMINATION

"One option is to self-destruct, wallow in self-pity, make excuses, and point fingers at the culprit. The other option is to learn from the event, permit it to enhance your skills, and build stronger perseverance and character."
—Marshall M. Baker

ON DEALING WITH CAREER TRANSITIONS

"Every leader needs to be repotted periodically if he or she is to remain effective. Repotting changes your perspective, enhances your toolbox, and renews your spirit."
—Thomas C. Royer

ON THE DOWNSIDE OF MAKING A CAREER CHANGE

"At least once during your career, it's highly likely that you and the organization will not be a good fit."
—Sherry A. Gentry

"Balance in one's life is crucial, and recognizing that opportunities emerge when you least expect them will be helpful in overcoming the frequent challenges during one's career."

—Gary S. Kaplan

ON WHAT'S NEEDED TO KEEP YOUR FOCUS ON A DREAM

"A clear sense of vision and mission . . . [and] a willingness to risk failure." —Edward A. Eckenhoff

ON ECONOMICS

"Don't be mesmerized by money. Sometimes a high salary may be a way of enticing you into a job with substantial flaws."

—Sherry A. Gentry

ON TECHNOLOGY

"Healthcare executives who do not realize IT's potential in their field will be unable to effectively incorporate technology into their organizational strategy."

—Thomas C. Dolan

ON MENTORS

"They can serve as sources of knowledge, and provide us with frank, unfiltered feedback and support. To be optimally effective, a mentor needs to be committed to work improvement and find personal satisfaction in this role." —Gary S. Kaplan

ON WHAT'S NEEDED TO MAKE THE DREAM A REALITY

"Be willing to change the course along which you will travel to get to your final destination, and be open to letting your vision evolve."

—Edward A. Eckenhoff

"The best work happens at the intersections of collaboration—where the talents, creativity, and experience of each discipline converge."
—Donald M. Berwick

ON AVOIDING FAILURE

"Above all, fear complacency."   —Edward A. Eckenhoff

ON WHAT MAKES A SUCCESSFUL CAREER

"Dedication to the task at hand, luck, and timing."
—David M. Lawrence

ON HOW TO GAUGE SUCCESS

"At the end of the day, we should each be judged by not only *what* we have accomplished, individually and as a team, but also *how* we accomplished it."   —Marshall M. Baker

While the career paths of each of these illustrious individuals are vastly different, it is clear that their common focus has been on the most important task of their chosen profession: finding ways to contribute to the process of caring for patients. It seems remarkable that none of these leaders evaluated their success in terms of profits or losses, the amount of income they generated, or their own personal celebrity. Rather, their satisfaction seems to have been generated by not compromising their integrity, perseverance in working toward team goals, visionary thinking, and hard work.

When the inevitable random events encroached on their turf, these leaders used them in a constructive way to learn, improve, and move forward. Their attention seems to have always been focused on creating a positive future for their organizations rather than on what was good for them personally. Maybe this is why their careers have been so easily distinguishable from the pack!

Careers

Marshall M. Baker, FACMPE

YOU REALLY DISCOVER things about your strength of character when you get fired. This sentinel moment can take you in one of two directions. One option is to self-destruct, wallow in self-pity, make excuses, and point fingers at the culprits. The other option is to learn from the event, permit it to enhance your skills, and build stronger perseverance and character.

In mid-career, I was fired from my job. I had served as the administrator of a multispecialty medical group for eight years. Being fired was a turning point in my life.

We had a section of dynamic surgeons within the group. Now, those of us who have worked with physicians, especially surgeons, are prone to stereotype their personalities. I realize that this is not particularly fair, but it's amazing how true to form stereotyping can sometimes be. From a medical perspective, our surgeons were excellent clinicians, respected and skilled in their field. However, they were also very aggressive and highly opinionated about everything. Moreover, they were typically accustomed to getting their way—right now!

As we concluded a financially challenging year, several surgeons came to me and sought my endorsement for borrowing money to pay year-end bonuses. Our compensation plan was based on charges, not collections, so while the money had been earned, our cash position would not allow for a payment without borrowing. Borrowing to pay bonuses was not a practical business decision. Consequently, I told them that I could not support their request.

The matter was elevated to the board of directors. I made the case for denying the request and the board accepted the argument. The loan was not sought.

Within three weeks, I was told that the group had made a decision to make a change in management and that I could collect my personal belongings and leave immediately. The group was true to my contract and I received the severance that was defined in my agreement.

Later I learned that several surgeons had flexed their muscle and lobbied that I be fired. Secret meetings were held at the homes of several of the physicians, all intended to oust me as the manager of the group. It is amazing how intimidated individuals and medical groups can become when high dollar producers threaten to leave if they don't get their way. The genuflecting to those individuals can be almost ludicrous, yet sad for the group at the same time.

I think back on this event and find peace in knowing that it was not a mistake, but a valuable learning experience. I wish I had been more perceptive about the political environment, but I confess I would make the same decision today.

I read a book recently by Spencer Johnson entitled, *Who Moved My Cheese?* The author talked about the importance of reading the handwriting on the wall. I clearly did not read that handwriting. Instead I stayed true to my values and I am a better person today from the lessons learned.

With respect to the lessons, there are a couple that really stand out. The first relates to the mental preparation for being fired. I have known some really fine managers who have been "excused" from medical groups over the years. These were talented professionals with terrific skills. However, events and individuals create situations that take down even the best. Strength of character and perseverance are the ingredients for surviving such an event. Those who persevere are the ones who, a year later, feel they are better off than before. I admire those professionals.

A second lesson is that it is critical to build and nurture the physician/administrator team relationship. Ultimately, trust is the single most important ingredient to the maintenance of an effective team. You must, however, work on it each day, protect it at all costs, and realize that you can lose it much faster than you can earn it. Once lost, it is difficult to earn it back. The essentials of developing trust within the team include the need for ongoing, open dialogue. Communications is fundamental and must not be neglected. A critical success factor is a performance evaluation process that is dynamic and constructive. Managers need to know where they stand in order to ensure there are no surprises. In a very real sense, performance evaluation is another means of communication.

I've had friends in the profession who professed that building friendships with the physicians they work with is important. Yet, it is rare when I have found a physician who truly sought out a personal relationship with me; many feel they are in a "different club" than me. I can live with that, as long as effective communication is accomplished at the right level. I have sought (and found) physicians and medical groups during my career where communication was open, trust did exist, and we did function as members of the same team. In fact, one of the proudest moments for me was when the physicians in a group where I was the executive publicly introduced me as "one of our partners."

At the end of the day, we should each be judged by not only what we have accomplished, individually and as a team, but also by how we have accomplished it.

Mr. Baker is the president and CEO *of Physician Advisory Services, Inc., in Boise, Idaho and was president of the American College of Medical Practice Executives in 1990.*

Careers

Donald M. Berwick, M.D.

DURING A WORKING lifetime, we are all faced with difficult decisions. The issue may involve strategy or logistics; it may be financial or operations related; or quite often it will be tied to career or personal objectives. Whatever the subject, the common denominator is that these decisions all entail some element of risk.

My toughest decision involved a change of careers in 1990 when I left a comfortable and secure position as vice president of Harvard Community Health Plan to become the full-time president and CEO of the Institute for Healthcare Improvement.

During my ten years with the Harvard plan, we continually worked to improve the processes of care delivery, but were more focused on measurement than actually improving the quality of care. Because of my keen interest in the care delivery process, I participated with several other concerned individuals to explore the development of a nonprofit organization dedicated to "accelerating improvement in healthcare systems by fostering collaboration, rather than competition, among healthcare organizations." Eventually, with the support of a three-year, $1,200,000 grant, the Institute for Healthcare Improvement was created.

The organization was small, and I agreed to become the part-time chief executive, while retaining my position with the HMO. As the activities of the Institute expanded, it became apparent that the CEO position needed full-time energy. It was the organization's first operational crisis and a personal decision point for me. I had to decide if I should leave the safe harbor of a known and respected position for a small, academic nonprofit enterprise with no track record and an unpredictable future.

I first considered the social and economic impact on my family. They were fully supportive of the move because of my passion for quality healthcare. Second, I considered the potential loss of prestige that accompanied the position at Harvard Community Health Plan. It was important, but not enough to dissuade me from making the change. Third, I considered the likelihood that the Institute could survive, and indeed thrive, over the long term. As I thought through the decision, two things came to mind. I knew that I believed in the mission of the new organization and its quest for meaningful social change, and I had faith that we could develop an agenda and services that would have a positive impact on improving the health status in America.

I made the move in 1991 and immediately began the process of organizational development.

In the first few months, we held visioning and planning sessions with many healthcare experts to help us create a strategic plan for the organization. At the same time, we set about building an infrastructure with the resources to support our educational and research missions. We also began the process of constructing programs that could generate enough revenue to sustain the Institute when the grant expired.

By 1994, we were financially viable and began the transition from a boutique-type organization to a professionally respected healthcare enterprise. The hiring of a very talented senior executive in 1995 invigorated that process.

Today, the Institute for Healthcare Improvement is a respected resource in the movement to fundamentally change healthcare delivery, and is consulted by business, government, and healthcare leaders from around the world. We see evidence every day that we are making substantial progress toward our stated goals of:

- improved health status,
- better clinical outcomes,
- reduced costs that do not compromise quality,

- greater access to care,
- an easier-to-use healthcare system, and
- improved satisfaction for patients and communities.

Our constant challenge is to continue providing bridges that connect organizations and people who are committed to real healthcare reform and who believe they can accomplish more by working together than they can separately.

My message to healthcare executives is that you must be interested in something bigger than yourself. The healthcare system is hungry for collaboration, and desperately needs leaders who are motivated to go beyond the everyday tasks of managing one organization and will use their imagination to find ways to contribute to the overall improvement of healthcare delivery and health status. My specific observations about how to accomplish this lofty goal are that:

- You must park your ego and degrees at the door before you begin work each day so that you can be open minded and team oriented.
- You must believe in the power and energy of collaboration and invite others to join the campaign for better healthcare.
- You must refuse to be smothered by conventional thinking, and embrace risk and change as a necessary part of leadership.
- You must remember that the best work happens at the intersections of collaboration—where the talents, creativity, and experience of each discipline and its people converge.

Dr. Berwick is the president and CEO *of the Institute for Healthcare Improvement in Boston, Massachusetts.*

Careers

Thomas C. Dolan, Ph.D., FACHE, CAE

WHEN I TALK to my colleagues who are my age and older—many of whom are senior executives—I am always concerned about those who say they believe they do not need to learn about personal computers and other information technology. When I first began my career in healthcare management, technological savvy was a good skill to have, but it was far from crucial. In today's knowledge- and information-oriented environment, however, my information technology skills have become as important to my ability to lead effectively as any other skill.

Most major functions of management are now driven, at least in part, by information technology. The cost, clinical, and other data required in our current environment are provided by increasingly powerful information systems, online technology, and personal computers. Healthcare executives today must be comfortable using these tools in our day-to-day decision making and communication, as well as understand some of the larger technology issues facing our organizations and the healthcare management field. Individuals who are not at ease obtaining information from sources such as these will find themselves and their organizations at a competitive disadvantage.

I have also found that comfort with tools such as e-mail has improved my ability to communicate with staff and colleagues. Some senior managers rely on assistants to handle all their e-mail communications, but by doing so, they lose the primary benefits of e-mail—its speed and spontaneity. Most younger professionals, on the other hand, are familiar with and quite at ease with the Internet and e-mail; many even prefer e-mail for business communication. The diverse demographic groups within an organization must learn to communicate by each other's preferred means; so just as younger executives must develop their verbal communication skills, senior executives need to know how to communicate via e-mail. As CEO, I can help set an example of this type of cooperation by demonstrating my own willingness to use e-mail and similar tools.

My awareness of technology has also been valuable in my supervision of IT staff. In most organizations, the chief information officer used to report to the chief financial officer, but as technology takes a greater role in overall business strategy, it is increasingly common for the CIO to report to the COO or CEO. To be able to adequately supervise the IT function, a COO or CEO must understand its capabilities. Healthcare executives who do not realize IT's potential in their field will be unable to effectively incorporate technology into their organizational strategy.

An understanding of IT's uses and applications is important even if the organization brings in outside consultants for technology projects. I was once involved in a major systems conversion in which we hired good IT consultants, but their strength was in general business—they had little experience in the specific activities of my type of organization. What they produced was a modified business system, not a system that was designed from the ground up for our specialized needs. I quickly learned that this new system did not effectively serve my staff or our customers, and therefore had been a waste of our time and resources. Now, I always make sure that any IT consultants we hire have ample experience with organizations like ours.

As a CEO with wide-ranging responsibilities, I certainly do not consider myself an expert in information technology. However, I find that I can stay on top of developments in this area by skimming publications such as *Healthcare Informatics*. In addition, I periodically attend conferences or similar events with the CIO and other technology staff. This gives us the opportunity to discuss current IT challenges, as well as work together in an educational setting to learn skills and strategies for addressing those challenges.

Finally, my organization's coo and I ensure that we are dedicating enough resources to IT training. Many organizations fail to do so—and this shortcoming is compounded by the fact that because of their expertise, IT staff often underestimate the amount of training non-IT staff require. For an organization to use technology effectively, senior management must provide the necessary tools to ensure success.

The field of healthcare management is becoming increasingly dependent on information technology, and this trend shows no signs of slowing down. Familiarity with IT tools, strategies, and challenges are now and will continue to be vital to healthcare executives' career success.

Dr. Dolan is president of the American College of Healthcare Executives in Chicago, Illinois.

Careers

Edward A. Eckenhoff, FACHE

MY GRAND ADVENTURE began in 1982. I was the 39-year-old vice president of administration at the Rehabilitation Institute of Chicago, thought by many to be the most prestigious rehabilitation hospital in the United States. Although my prospects for succeeding eventually to the presidency were excellent, I resolved to relinquish that secure job and promising future for a more challenging opportunity.

I decided to build a comprehensive rehabilitation hospital where there was none—right in the heart of the nation's capital, Washington, DC. This was not my dream alone. I partnered with three real estate developers who brought to the table most of the cash. I contributed some funds, but my greatest asset was my professional expertise in managing a medical rehabilitation institution.

In Washington, local providers were not meeting the needs of people who had experienced disabling injuries and illnesses. Though there were departments at area hospitals that delivered rehabilitation care, local residents could only obtain the gamut of medical rehabilitation services by leaving town and, in some cases, traveling great distances. Those with spinal cord and traumatic brain injuries were being sent to rehabilitation facilities in Pennsylvania or Connecticut, even to Chicago, hundreds of miles away from family and friends at a time when they most needed their support and attention.

As a professional, I was both appalled by this healthcare gap and excited about the prospect of plugging it. On a personal level, I could empathize with those whose care was being shortchanged solely because of where they happened to live, for I, too, had experienced a disabling injury as a young man.

My dream was to develop a national model of excellence in the field of medical rehabilitation and call it the National Rehabilitation Hospital (NRH). I also eventually envisioned expanding it from a stand-alone hospital to a multi-institutional specialty healthcare system. The reality turned out to be quite different than I would ever have imagined, though no less interesting or rewarding than I anticipated. "Rewarding" may seem an odd way to describe it, for I nearly went bankrupt in the process.

While preparing for our move to Washington, DC, my wife Judi and I knew exactly six people in the nation's capital—my three partners and their spouses. When we were discussing whether to pull up stakes in Chicago, I remember her saying: "Let's give it a try. If it doesn't work out, I can always go back to being a therapist. You can go back to being a director of admitting and work your way up the ladder again." My wife's support and willingness to take a chance—a sentiment that mirrored mine—made this *our* adventure and helped me to keep things in perspective as the partnership's debts piled up into the millions of dollars (courtesy of architects, lawyers, consultants, land payments, and interest on bank loans).

Some healthcare providers were worried that we would steal their patients and decrease their bed utilization. There were also doctors who could not understand how a specialty hospital would work. Worse, they had the ear of political decision makers. We were in danger of going under while we struggled to get our certificate of need. After many a day and night spent with politicians, physicians, and hospital administrators who were skeptical about what we were going to build, we did acquire our certificate of need.

We were saved from bankruptcy by the Washington Healthcare Corporation (WHCC), a nonprofit multi-institutional system that included the largest acute care hospital in the area. After discussions that led to our being purchased by WHCC, the debts of the partnership were paid and I was hired as the president of the yet-to-be built rehabilitation hospital. This was a critical turning point. Eighteen months after we took in that first patient, our revenues began to exceed expenses. Ever since then, we have always had a profitable year. In 14 years, we have grown to a comprehensive medical rehabilitation system with a $100 million operating budget.

Flexibility continues to be one of our hallmarks. Faced with relentless pressures from managed care to shorten lengths of stay for our inpatients, we moved expeditiously to bolster the outpatient end of the continuum of care for our patient population. Over the course of several years we have expanded an ambulatory network from a handful of sites to nearly three dozen.

Previously I had thought our missions were delivering quality care to patients, providing top-notch education and training to students and staff, and engaging in substantive rehabilitation research. Eventually, we came to realize that for our comprehensive medical rehabilitation hospital, those three missions would not suffice. So we added two more: rehabilitation engineering (providing assistive technology for our patients) and advocacy for people with disabilities.

Today NRH boasts one of the finest assistive technology and rehabilitation research programs in the country and, in the Washington metropolitan area, is the dominant force in specialty training for rehabilitation professionals. NRH has entered into formal partnerships with the Warren Grant Magnuson Clinical Center at the National Institutes of Health and several suburban hospitals. NRH is consistently ranked in the *U.S. News & World Report* "Best Hospitals" list as one of the top rehabilitation hospitals in the country and is always the youngest such facility on the list.

I wish that I could say that all this came to pass through some grand scheme. It did not. The development of NRH took on a life of its own and was both a wondrous and humbling lesson for me. I came to realize that, as the founder, I was little more than someone who had an idea and possessed enough sense to pick people brighter than I was and to give them the responsibility to transform my idea into something bigger and better than I had ever imagined. All that NRH is today is the result of hundreds of individuals who were given ownership in developing a piece of my dream.

As I think back on my life-altering decision in 1982, three important lessons come to mind. First, if you have a vision and decide to pursue it, be willing to change the course along which you will travel to get to your final estination. Be open to letting your vision evolve. Second, surround yourself with the brightest people you can to help you meet your goals. Third, above all, fear complacency. No one wishes to fail, but you are truly defeated only if you go down while taking refuge in holding patterns and the status quo.

Mr. Eckenhoff is the CEO of National Rehabilitation Hospital in Washington, DC and was a member of the American Hospital Association board of trustees from 1990 to 1993.

Careers

Sherry A. Gentry, FACMPE

It is a rare occurrence today for a medical executive to remain with the same organization for his or her entire career. In fact, most executives look upon periodic change as healthy and desirable because it affords opportunities for increased responsibility, more income, and a chance to expand skills and knowledge. But there *is* a down side. At least once during your career, it is highly likely that you and the organization will not be a good fit. My advice is to deal with this situation in a positive way and try to gain as much as you can from the experience.

I spent the early years of my career with two small medical groups before I took a position as administrative director of satellites for Virginia Mason Medical Center in Seattle. This was a large physician-owned practice with wonderful values and a passion for its mission. There were strong peer relationships, an excellent communications network, and a nurturing spirit that fostered loyalty and enthusiasm.

During my seven years with vmmc, I sharpened my problem-solving skills, I became a competent team member, and I learned how to deal with adversity. Most importantly, however, I was given the chance to mature my management and leadership philosophy.

I left the organization when I got married and moved to another state.

My new employer was a large, respected hospital system that had recently organized several primary care practices into a group and had sponsored an ipa. I was the executive director of both the

25-physician group and 100-physician IPA. An outside consultant had been running the group on an interim basis. I was pleased with the stated values of the system, as well as the system's CEO. She was young, energetic, and bright, and I felt that we could work together very comfortably. I did recognize some organizational confusion during the interview process, but the money was very good, and I felt that I could work through any initial problems that might arise.

It only took a short time to realize that the operating philosophy of the hospital system was much different than I was used to, and that physicians were looked upon much differently than at Virginia Mason. While the CEO seemed to value the role of physicians, many of the subordinate managers did not. The pervading feeling was that physicians were more of an inconvenience than members of a healthcare team, and often the relationships between primary care physicians, specialists, and administrators were adversarial. Because of my past experience and orientation, I concluded that I was not a good fit for the organization. I had only been there a few months, so I decided that the best course of action for me was to work for positive change.

I spent the next two and a half years in trying to sort out roles; clarify responsibilities; design basic operating systems, processes, and standards; improve communications between the medical staff and administrators; and reorient the organization as best I could. There was much angst among the staff because we always seemed to be moving from one crisis to another.

Finally, a decision was made to employ our CPA firm to conduct an operations audit and provide feedback that might help improve attitudes and redirect the organization's culture.

The company was a "big six firm" with long-term ties to the hospital system. In my opinion, they correctly identified the issues, but because they did not want to jeopardize their relationship with the system, they chose to ignore or obscure the root culture problems that existed. I had high hopes that the audit would have a meaningful effect in making positive change. Unfortunately, it didn't, and I then realized that it was time for me to move on.

I was much more careful as I looked for a new employer, and my diligence paid off. I found Presbyterian Health Services in Albuquerque, New Mexico, whose operating philosophy and values very closely matched my own. The organization has a strong vision, a sense of group practice, and a passion to serve the community. It is now a pleasure to go to work each day.

In the ideal world, we would never have a negative work experience. However, we don't live in a utopia, so the best thing to do is learn from our mistakes. While I certainly wouldn't want to repeat those three frustrating years, I must admit that I learned a great deal that I might not otherwise have been exposed to if I had stayed in my previous job. Those lessons have been valuable in expanding my knowledge base and confirming my leadership philosophy. Here are a few of those lessons:

- The right fit is critical to career satisfaction and a sense of accomplishment.
- One shouldn't feel guilty or inadequate when they make a wrong career choice. We all do it. The challenge is to recognize the poor fit and move on as soon as it makes sense.
- Successful medical organizations have strong physician leadership and a sense of partnership with administrative leaders.
- Don't be mesmerized by money. Sometimes a high salary may be a way of enticing you into a job with substantial flaws. Most organizations know when things aren't right, and they try to cover up the realities by offering lots of money to recruit strong management.
- Remember that you can learn from every experience, even adverse ones. You can always use them as bad examples!

Ms. Gentry is the executive director of operations for Presbyterian Healthcare Services in Albuquerque, New Mexico and was president of the American College of Medical Practice Executives in 1999.

Careers

Gary S. Kaplan, M.D., CMPE

I ATTENDED MEDICAL school at the University of Michigan and completed a general internal medicine residency at Virginia Mason Medical Center in Seattle, Washington. The memories of my training are mostly positive, primarily because of the wonderful people in the organization who were committed to education.

During this time, I was fortunate to be mentored by several very talented professionals. As I was completing my training and looking for my first job, I was encouraged by the organization's leadership to apply for an attending physician position in our downtown general internal medicine office. As a result of this encouragement, I was optimistic that I would be offered this job and focused my long-term career planning around this opportunity. Due to conflicting needs and deferring interests between the members of the group and the overall organization, I was not offered the position. This was devastating for me personally and professionally. My ego and professional confidence were temporarily wounded as a result of this major disappointment. I learned many lessons as a result.

During this time, my family and friends were extremely supportive. Professionally, individuals who had served as my mentors during my training within the organization provided great perspective and professional focus that clearly kept me on track and helped me take advantage of the next opportunity.

Soon thereafter, I learned of the activities of Virginia Mason Medical Center, a $500 million integrated delivery system with 400 physicians, a 336-bed, acute-care hospital, 16 regional facilities, and 3,500 employees. The Center was embarking on a new venture in regional clinic development and I was asked to take on a clinical and leadership role in this development work. This represented an outstanding opportunity and subsequently has led to the development of new skills, knowledge, and abilities working in leadership roles with diverse individuals facing both management and clinical challenges.

It is rare that professionals go through their lives without experiencing some element of disappointment, failure, and setback. These may be devastating for high-powered individuals who have experienced minimal failures in the past.

There are several lessons and opportunities that can emerge from the experience of disappointment and temporary failure. These experiences can help mold a successful professional career. Maintenance of optimism in spite of failure is an important attribute for those who become successful leaders. The ability to understand that learning is often achieved because of adversity and disappointment can be an important sustaining ingredient for a strong leader. Even at times of great challenge, successful leaders are able to keep things in perspective. Balance in one's life is crucial, and recognizing that opportunities emerge when you least expect them will be helpful in overcoming the frequent challenges during one's career.

I came to learn that I had definite opportunities to move in a variety of directions. I have often thought about the human stem cell, which has the potential to differentiate in a variety of different cell lines, and that this biological model is analogous to the human potential. Mid-course corrections are often necessary to optimally develop during one's professional career. The ability to be nimble and flexible while maintaining focus, energy, and optimism can be important ingredients for the successful leader.

Perhaps the greatest learning has been an understanding of the role of mentors and role models. They often are people who have "been there and done that." They can serve as sources of knowledge and frank, unfiltered feedback and support. To be optimally effective, a mentor needs to be committed to improvement work and find personal satisfaction in this role. Formalizing the process of selecting a mentor is challenging and should be done with great care. Committed mentoring relationships can be extremely powerful and effective. As the challenges in healthcare increase and adversarial interactions emerge, long-standing trusting relationships will be sustaining and essential to organizational success.

I am the beneficiary of effective mentoring and am committed to using my experience to facilitate the development of young, energetic individuals looking to find their niche and fulfill their potential. We must find the people with the energy and passion to promote our organizational growth, development, and tough decision making. They must be receptive to feedback and we, as leaders, must be committed to their success. By working to understand our own experiences, we will be best able to prepare our future leaders to develop professionally and contribute to their organization's success.

Dr. Kaplan is the chairman and CEO *of Virginia Mason Medical Center in Seattle, Washington and is the board chair of the Medical Group Management Association for 2001.*

Careers

David M. Lawrence, M.D.

ONE OF THE most common questions asked by young medical executives is, "How do I plan my career?" My answer is, "You don't."

There is too much uncertainty, luck, fate, and randomness to allow anyone to accurately plot the course of their career from start to finish. While job performance is certainly critical to success, career paths are also very dependent on organizational culture, working relationships, the outside environment, and just plain good timing.

It is certainly natural to think about managing one's career. However, my advice is not to think one step ahead while you're trying to fulfill the responsibilities of your current position. The reason is that you aren't likely to give your job the time and attention necessary to excel, and too often you'll take actions and make decisions based on where you want to go instead of what your organization needs. That can be very debilitating. On the other hand, it's very liberating not to worry about what comes next.

I suggest that the best way to assure a successful career is to focus exclusively on the job at hand, being as creative and vigorous as possible. Set performance goals for yourself and work diligently to achieve them. Explore your talents, develop your skills, and learn more about the world around you. Absorb all you can from the organization, the industry, and the outside environment. The experience you gain from the job will allow you to grow and be better prepared when opportunity knocks.

Remember that you can't predict when opportunity will call, so don't set arbitrary timetables for advancement. Just be prepared when the time comes. Most people will eventually feel that they have accomplished their mission in a given position and will begin to feel a sense of restlessness. When that happens, it's wise to begin searching for other positions either within or outside the organization. When evaluating your alternatives, look for positions that you'll enjoy, as well as ones that will offer you new challenges. Once you take the job, repeat the process. Performance, timing, and fate will take care of the next step.

This process worked successfully for me several times in my career.

Many years ago when I was in my early forties, I was the Portland County Health Officer responsible for Human Services. I enjoyed the job, and really had no plans to move until my boss, the county executive, made a decision to run for governor of Oregon. It was then that I sensed that restlessness, and began thinking of looking for a new job.

Almost out of the blue, I received a call from Kaiser Permanente in Portland, and eventually was offered a position as vice president for medical operations. I became chief of staff of the hospital, as well as area director. That change was purely random.

Five years later, I was beginning to feel that I had accomplished my mission and began thinking about making a change. Once again, fate intervened. Completely unexpectedly, I was offered the chance to become the CEO of Kaiser Colorado Health Plan. That required a major family move and an opportunity to expand my knowledge and experience.

Over time, that move led to the position I now hold.

In summary, a successful career is the product of dedication to the task at hand, luck, and timing.

If you apply yourself to each job properly, the journey will be exhilarating and challenging because of the opportunities to learn. My advice is to follow your instincts, be open to the possibilities, and have lots of "ah-ha's!" along the way.

Dr. Lawrence is the chairman and CEO *of Kaiser Foundation Health Plan, Inc., in Oakland, California.*

Careers

Thomas C. Royer, M.D.

WHEN I COMPLETED my surgical residency and joined the medical staff of the Geisinger Medical Center in 1974, it never occurred to me that my role in medicine might change through the years, or that I would one day actually leave the organization altogether. I certainly had no reason to think I would gradually assume more and more administrative and leadership responsibilities, and would eventually be transformed into a full-fledged medical executive. It took many years to comprehend that this metamorphosis was taking place.

As I began to realize after 17 years that I was not being stretched intellectually, and was not fully utilizing my talents, I had to make a choice. I could either accept the loss of energy and enthusiasm as an inevitable consequence of life and work or I could decide to reinvigorate my career by moving to a new organization.

As painful as it was to contemplate, I knew it must be done. On the one hand, I was an established leader in the organization, I was competent in my functional areas, and I had comfortable ties to my neighbors, colleagues, and the community. On the other hand, I felt that I was beginning to stagnate and needed new daily challenges. As disconcerting and challenging as it was to my family and me, I chose the path to broaden my career horizons.

It turned out to be a wise choice.

I accepted a position in a new city with more responsibility and new challenges. My new position with the Johns Hopkins Services

Corporation was very energizing and fulfilling. I had a chance to broaden my skills and truly affect the culture and operation of a new organization.

Two years later, I was approached by another well-known and highly respected health system and offered an opportunity to grow even more. While I was satisfied with my position and felt that there were still many more contributions I could make, I once again chose to move. I did so because the new position at Henry Ford Health System gave me responsibilities in all three areas of medicine—clinical, education, and research—as opposed to just the clinical area in the current position. While I had concerns about leaving after only two years, and I knew I would miss the friendships and associations I had developed, the decision was far less painful than my previous move.

I enjoyed my five years at Henry Ford immensely. We made major strides as an organization, and I learned much from my colleagues, mentors, and the organization itself. While I had many opportunities to guide the direction and culture of the system through my position as the chief medical officer and chairman of the board of the medical group, I ultimately wanted the chance to be chief executive officer of a substantial healthcare system. Because of my many years' association with three respected systems, I was afforded that opportunity in late 1999.

I relate that chronology so that you can understand the framework for my comments about transitions. Leaving one job and moving to another is a vital and enriching experience. It is certainly not without some measure of trauma, but it clearly provides a path to grow, to renew, and to broaden your skill and knowledge base. My observations and advice about transitions are these:

- When you sense that you're becoming more about maintenance than innovation, it's time to look for a new opportunity.
- Recognize that changing jobs will disrupt your personal and professional networks and will put stress on you and your family. It will be particularly intense with the first move.
- Also recognize that a new job in a new organization is typically

energizing and stimulating, and generally offers a great chance to learn and add new skills for your management/leadership toolbox.

- Be sure you move for the right reasons. Find an organization where you can utilize your talents effectively, and exercise some influence over the culture and fabric of the new enterprise.
- Before you accept the new position, you must ask yourself these questions:
  – Do I have the energy to start over?
  – Do I have the energy and commitment to build a new team?
  – Do I have the energy to infuse the new organization with enthusiasm and confidence?
  – Do I have the energy to create an appropriate strategic direction for the new organization?
- Be sure you do a thorough job of due diligence about the organization before you accept the offer. Look carefully at its clinical operation, fiscal performance, and potential; its commitment to its team; and the strength of its current leadership. Also understand, to the degree possible, its challenges.
- Understand that you really have two jobs from the moment you accept a new position until you actually join the new enterprise. From the notice period to joining your current employer, you must work extra hard to fulfill your responsibilities well, while beginning the orientation period for your new position. It will be a strenuous four- to six-month period in your life.

I personally found that transitions gave me added confidence, provided avenues to demonstrate new capabilities, reinvigorated me, and ultimately made me a better leader. Because every organization has its own unique culture, values, strategy, and tactics, they provided excellent venues for "pulling my experience forward" and testing the validity of my leadership style.

Perhaps the most important lesson I've learned from my career transitions is that every leader needs to be repotted periodically if he or she is to remain effective. Repotting changes your perspective, enhances your toolbox, and renews your spirit—not unlike the passage from winter to spring. Transition means risk, but calculated risk taking offers great rewards. It has worked for me. Done correctly, it should work for you, too.

Dr. Royer is the president and CEO *of Christus Health System in Irving, Texas. He was a board member of the Medical Group Management Association from 1994 to 1999, and currently serves on the American Hospital Association Board of Trustees and the Executive Committee.*

Careers

Frederick J. Wenzel, FACMPE

In 1976 I was the executive director of the Marsh-field Medical Foundation for Research and Education in Marshfield, Wisconsin. I had been a researcher transformed into a manager. The foundation served as the research arm of the Marshfield Clinic and, I confess, we served in the shadows of the clinic.

The Clinic stood on the threshold of major change and growth. Approximately 140 physicians worked at the clinic at that time. As with many medical groups, it struggled with finding the right person to lead the organization in the senior most administrative capacity. There were several years where the clinic transitioned through a couple of very fine individuals who did not possess the skill sets necessary to take the institution to the next level. It is not that these individuals were incapable of leading, they just did not have the right chemistry for Marshfield at the time.

I recall attending a meeting of the clinic executive committee one afternoon. I was always invited as a guest to those meetings as well as the meetings of the board. Following a lengthy executive session during which time we guests were excused, I was summoned back into the boardroom and they offered me the position of chief executive officer. I found it curious that they would not do a national search, but instead would offer the job to someone with experience as a research administrator. After all, what did I know of managing a medical group practice?

The answer to the question came in the form of three observations from the president and the committee members.

1. I knew the physicians and had genuine respect for their work.
2. The physicians had developed a confidence in my motives and my work. They appreciated my work ethic and they trusted that I had the passion to do the right things for the group. They knew that I was not a self-serving leader.
3. They observed that my heart and soul was always in my work. Ultimately, they felt that the quest I had for quality performance, both in the organization and in myself, was an enduring characteristic that was important for the group's development.

Over the years that I was with Marshfield Clinic, I worked with six physician presidents. Moreover, we expanded and grew to nearly 500 physicians in 28 satellite offices, and we developed a successful HMO and a large regional laboratory service.

Teaching is my passion today. I now have students seeking advice regarding career paths and successful professional fits. I encourage students to do self-assessments of their talents, skills, and values. I ask them the question, "How do you define success and what will it take for you to get there?"

It is important to define the type of environment and the value system of the people with whom you work. When looking for the right situation, be yourself and assess if the organization appreciates your talents and personality. Also, don't forget to ask a lot of questions of those empowered in the organization to make sure it's a fit for you. Every opportunity is not a good one.

I've thought a lot about balancing ambition and ethics. On the one hand, there is much to be said for the individual who strives to achieve excellence in their work. There is absolutely nothing wrong in having career goals toward which you strive. However, although achievements and accomplishments are noble, they should not be at the expense of compromising your ethical standards and your values. To the extent an organization ranks success higher than the ethical standards by which they are attained, it's not an organization for which you would want to work.

I have always been a competitor and achiever. I consider a challenge part of the fuel that makes life so energizing and fun. So my family did not find it a surprise when I started mountain climbing several years ago. As with most challenges in my life, I took the sport on with a vengeance. I have stepped on the summit of Mt. Adams, Mt. Hood, Mt. St. Helen's, Mt. Rainer, Mt. Whitney, Mt. Kilimanjaro, and about 20 of Colorado's "14'ers" (mountains with peaks that are at or over 14,000 feet high). Each adventure brought a unique set of challenges that had to be overcome in order to be successful in navigating to the summit.

As a team organizes a climb, the positioning of each individual is critical. The route finder takes the lead. This is the person who chooses the path most likely to lead to success. It's a job that takes intuition, experience, and decisiveness. The strongest individual in the party must fill the end position on the team. This is the person of last resort if there is an accident and one of the members falls. This is a job that requires quickness, sureness of foot, and endurance. All of the climbers in the middle positions depend on each other to transfer information and assist with anchoring. Everyone on the team has a role to play and the team is only as successful as the weakest link.

Such is also true of the team charged with managing a medical group practice. Each person has a job to perform, the sum of which is the positive and constructive impact on the group and how it translates to the success of the organization. As an individual seeks opportunities with groups, he or she should look for those teams where there is mutual respect, confidence, and a value system that is understood and cherished.

Mr. Wenzel is a professor and academic director at the University of St. Thomas in Minneapolis, Minnesota and was president of the American College of Medical Practice Executives in 1993.

About the Editors

DONALD J. LLOYD, FACMPE

Mr. Lloyd has been a noted healthcare leader and speaker on healthcare administration issues, managerial ethics, accountability, and healthcare policy for more than two and a half decades. He has also written extensively for various regional and national healthcare journals on these same topics. His first book, HEALTHCARE 2010: A Journey to the Past, chronicles the transformation of the healthcare system from managed care to a public utility.

Mr. Lloyd spent 24 years as a group practice executive with medical groups in California, Alabama, and Tennessee. During that time, he also served in many appointed and elected positions with local, state, regional, and national Medical Group Management Association chapters, serving as the national president in 1996. In addition, Mr. Lloyd has been an adjunct instructor for the University of Alabama at Birmingham and a preceptor for the University of Minnesota Independent Study Program. He has also held director positions for an offshore malpractice insurance company, two physician-owned independent practice associations, and a health maintenance organization.

In 1998, Mr. Lloyd cofounded The StarLight Group, a healthcare consulting company with offices in Atlanta and Nashville. He received his bachelor of business administration degree from the University of Georgia in 1967 and his master of business administration degree from Georgia State University in Atlanta in 1974. He was awarded

Fellow status in the American College of Medical Practice Executives in 1979.

DONALD C. WEGMILLER, FACHE

Mr. Wegmiller is president and chief executive officer of HealthCare Compensation Strategies (formerly MCG/HealthCare), a division of Clark/Bardes Holdings, Inc., a nationally recognized executive compensation firm focusing on large banks and public corporations.

Mr. Wegmiller brings more than 35 years of experience in healthcare administration to HealthCare Compensation Strategies, many spent managing multihospital systems. Prior to coming to HealthCare Compensation Strategies, he served as vice chairman and president of HealthSpan Health Systems Corporation, Minnesota's largest healthcare network.

Mr. Wegmiller has written and lectured extensively about a number of healthcare topics, and his work has been published in a variety of national healthcare publications. He currently teaches healthcare administration at the University of Minnesota, Duke University, and Arizona State University. From 1986 to 1988, Mr. Wegmiller served as a chairman officer of the American Hospital Association, serving in 1987 as the organization's chairman, the highest elected office. He also has been named a Fellow in the American College of Healthcare Executives. Mr. Wegmiller received both his bachelor's degree and master's degree in health administration from the University of Minnesota.

W. ROBERT WRIGHT, JR., FACMPE

Mr. Wright is an accomplished speaker and author on various management and leadership topics. The American College of Medical Practice Executives named him the Administrator of the Year in 1983, and he was the recipient of the Edward B. Stevens Article of the Year Award given by the ACMPE in 1995. His first book, *Going Places*, is a perspective on management, leadership, and the value of personal reflection in your career.

Throughout his career, Mr. Wright has served in many leadership positions, most notably as chair of the board of directors of the Medical Group Management Association in 1999, president of the Academic Practice Assembly of MGMA in 1997, and president of the American College of Medical Practice Executives in 1989.

Mr. Wright is the chief executive officer of The StarLight Group, a healthcare consulting company with offices in Nashville and Atlanta. Before cofounding The StarLight Group, he held management positions at the University of Alabama at Birmingham, Virginia Commonwealth University, the University of Virginia, and West Virginia University. He received his bachelor's degree from Auburn University and has completed graduate studies at the University of Alabama at Birmingham. He is also a Fellow in the American College of Medical Practice Executives.